2021 Cloud Guide

Using Cloud-Based Applications to Improve and Simplify Your Legal Practice

By: Andrew Zaso, CloudRDY LLC

TABLE OF CONTENTS

Introduction

This book is for everyone who has dreamed of using technology to automate their law firm's administrative functions. Cloud-based technologies offer many ways to operate your business without paying huge upfront technology costs. You can obtain technology that helps to level the playing field with your competitors for a small monthly subscription fee, thus lowering your operating costs. But where do you get started? Which tools are worth considering? How do you make the shift to using the cloud and use it safely? What exactly is the 'The Cloud," and how will it help your law practice?

Days of going to a physical office to conduct business are gone as the people demand the flexibility to work anytime from anywhere. The 'Gig' economy is service-based, where people get paid for the services they provide, not where the work occurs. This book aims to make the dreams of a flexible and mobile workplace possible for every person who works in the legal industry. This book is for anyone who wants to learn a new way to work and grow in today's economy.

Perhaps you have heard about the cloud and don't understand what it means. Everything you see and read tells you how the cloud can transform the way you work. But do you know the proper steps to get started? It is very confusing when you cannot see the big picture and how all the different parts connect. You are also probably wondering how the cloud can automate aspects of your legal practice, help you find new clients, and reduce your operating costs.

Let's start by dispelling a great marketing rumor; the cloud is not new. In the old days, computer services were all hosted on someone else's computer, which you accessed remotely. Do you remember when AOL provided email and connections to message boards through a modem connection - that was cloud computing. When your company sends your hours off to a company to calculate withholding, benefits, and send you a pay statement - that is cloud computing. Over the years, you may have adopted on-line banking where you access another computer to see your banking records - that is, cloud computing. Simply defined, cloud computing is using someone else's computer.

While the cloud concept is not new, what has changed is the ability to accomplish many administrative activities in the cloud at a low monthly cost. Now you can co-edit a document in the cloud, communicate with others through video conference applications, and have email. Your interactions with companies have changed where you now use corporate workflow to sign mortgage documents, book travel, and order products at any hour of the day. The cloud has increased your productivity while reducing dependency on human beings. People with the ability to navigate the cloud and use multiple cloud applications at the same time can achieve greater proficiencies, leverage their time better, and most importantly, save money. The cloud has grown into a game-changer for people and businesses willing to adapt and embrace new ways of working.

But, as you move your operations to the cloud, don’t forget about cloud security, as you are storing your critical business information on someone else's computer. Every day you read stories in the news about computer security hacks. Data about you or your company is vulnerable to bad actors trying to obtain that information and harm you. People make security decisions in the cloud that they would never make in real life. Would you walk around with just one key that opened your house, car, safety deposit box, etc.? Do you ignore the safety checks for your car, like checking the gas gauge each time you drive? What seems like basic common sense in real life is ignored in the cloud. This book will explore ways to keep you safe in the cloud and help you monitor your accounts for exploitation. Just like driving involves accepting risk, so is your life in the cloud. You must continuously be aware and mindful of how information can be gathered and used against you.

Lessons learned from COVID-19 can be seen in the growth of cloud technologies. Companies that embrace the cloud were able to adapt and survive. Those companies unable to adapt to the changes began to suffer. Think about how restaurants started offering their menus on your cell phone overnight, or how they could use the GPS on your phone to monitor how close you were to picking up your food, so it was ready when you arrived. Overnight the world changed, and so did the way companies operated. Adopting the cloud is no longer a decision to make in the future; it's about business survival today.

This book aims to help you build a secure platform for your life in the cloud, and then find applications that can enhance your legal practice. The cloud is an exciting place and represents so much potential for you personally and professionally. You can access information and learn in ways that were not previously possible. The cloud has made the world a smaller place and eliminated boundaries.

Because the applications and services available in the cloud are always changing, no single book can be a definitive guide. Instead, this book will identify some of the best applications available in different business categories to help in your decision process. I hope that this book gives you a basic understanding of the cloud and opens you to new tools that can help you be more productive personally and professionally.

The cloud has evolved into an exciting place where anything is possible. Let's get started!

Why You Need This Book

Most of the information in this book can be found on the internet, legal podcasts, blogs, and journals. The purpose of this book is to distill all that information into one place. We will start by discussing concepts about the cloud and then explore applications that can improve your law practice. The ideas presented here about the cloud can help you, and are evident in your daily life as you use cloud-based email, scheduling, banking, and other types of apps. This book allows you to put all the information you need at your fingertips in one easy guide.

Working in the cloud, or migrating to it, is not as easy as pulling a switch. Rather, the journey to operating in the cloud is a process filled with trial and error. It's a journey filled with steps that build upon each other. To successfully move to the cloud, you need to establish a foundation built on strong security practices. The next step is to automate workflows that are repeatable tasks within your business. You will quickly see the power of leveraging the cloud as it frees you from mundane tasks, allowing you to focus on your customer. If you don't build upon a strong foundation and a solid understanding of how your products integrate, the path you follow can be limited.

If you consider moving your law practice to the cloud as a project, then you need to consider the three factors that define every project:

Scope: This refers to the amount of work you want to move to the cloud. You may decide that you want to start by just moving your files to the cloud to protect them from any disasters that may impact your computer, such as a crashed hard drive, physical damage, or theft. You may want to move your scheduling or case management to the cloud, so you are no longer tied to a physical location, have 24 x 7 availability, and use the internet's automation power to supplement your staffing capabilities.

You do not need to tackle everything at once. With the right foundation in place, you can start with a limited scope addressing the most important items to you. Over time, you can add additional functions to your project. Each time you select a new cloud-based solution, you will need to evaluate how it integrates with the products you already use. We will show you how to do this in a logical progression of steps.

Money: The beauty of the cloud is that you get functioning and capabilities at a monthly rate, without having to spend large amounts of money to get started. Think about the costs, large law firms pay in user licenses, hardware costs, configuration, and maintenance every time they add a new computer system. The maintenance cost to compete these steps also costs money as implementing a new computer system can take months or years to do correctly. These companies are adopting huge applications that are designed and configured to how they work.

Cloud applications typically come with a monthly fee tied to the number of users. When you use cloud-based applications, you pay for exactly what you use. As your needs change, you have the flexibility to increase your licensing or product level to meet them. Of course, there are trade-offs in that you are limited in the configuration as you may need to adopt a new vocabulary or workflow to use a product. But, you benefit from using a program for which thousands of hours have gone into developing for a low monthly fee. If the program no longer meets your needs, you simply cancel your subscription. The risk you take on as a law firm in adopting new software is very little, as the upfront costs you pay are very low. Cloud-based applications level the playing field, allowing small firms to compete against larger firms with more resources.

Time: Want to try a new cloud-based application? Most cloud-based applications offer a free trial, so you can explore how their product operates. You do not need to purchase hardware to create a "Test Environment" or dedicate users as testers to conduct an evaluation. Instant access to new functionality is available in the cloud. And if something doesn't work the way you like, unsubscribe and try something new!

In your law firm, you know that time is money, and operating in the cloud affords you the ability to try new functionality at a very low cost. Every application works slightly differently, and you need to select the solution which best matches your business needs. Products that work well for one firm may not match your requirements, so consider recommendations but always try the cloud-based application out yourself. The time you spent in the evaluation process is minimal to its long term impact on your business.

You may be thinking this is great but is all this effort to change worth it? Let's face it, the old ways of operating may have served you well in the past, and considerable time and effort are involved in change. The time and effort to implement a new change takes you away from servicing your clients, which is why you are in business. Change also involves business risk as you step out of the known and into new ways of working.

Client satisfaction is the primary reason for the change. While there are many benefits you will achieve as a law firm by adopting cloud-based applications, your customers will also gain many benefits - and that is what matters. Think about it; your customers are used to working in a world where services are available 24 x 7. If you want to check your bank account, do you go to the physical bank and talk to the teller, or access your account from your smartphone? Do you go to the county building to pay your property tax, or do you log in at night and take care of your bill? Your customers are expecting the same type of 24 x 7 availability when they work with you. Many of these cloud-based applications provide customer portals for document management, appointment scheduling applications, and most importantly, payment applications. Today's clients expect service around the clock, and cloud-based applications make it possible for you to meet their expectations, even if you are a solo attorney.

Then there is the issue of your competitor. Have they already made the shift to integrating cloud-based applications in their legal practice? Can you compete with them if you are still using older technologies? If a client, as a consumer, had to choose between your firm and your competitor, who would they pick?

If a client cannot find information quickly on your website or access their case documents at night when they get home from work or learn the status of their cases 24 x 7, will they switch to another company? Accessibility is a component of service and how they judge your firm. In addition to accessibility, these tools also help you build a relationship with your clients, leading to additional work or more clients based on their referrals. Most importantly, adopting cloud services will help you shed the daily administrative tasks and give you more time to focus on what is important - helping your clients.

What is the Cloud

Let's start by defining the cloud. Merriam Webster dictionary defines cloud computing as:

"the practice of storing regularly used computer data on multiple servers that can be accessed through the internet"

This definition is very clear and concise. Using the cloud is about accessing resources through the internet. People who work in the technology industry like to define the cloud as using someone else's computer to accomplish a task using the cloud. Think about it, when you access anything through the internet, you are connecting to and using someone else's computer to achieve a task. 'Working in the Cloud' can mean storing files on a file server, accessing information from a web site, or using an application you access through the internet. Where that server resides and where the data is stored (in most cases) does not matter. Someone else has done all the work to set up the infrastructure, install and configure the application, and grant access to the application. Someone else is monitoring the application's performance, running backups, and installing patches.

Cloud services are available at three levels, and you can purchase any of them depending on your needs. Each layer has its benefits and issues which should be addressed. They can be divided up as follows:

IaaS - Infrastructure as a Service

Infrastructure refers to the physical items needed to run an application and usually fall into three categories: Servers, Storage, Network. When you think about a data center, you are looking at the infrastructure which makes applications work. The things you don't see are the costs associated with running infrastructures. These are the cost of building and maintaining the physical structure, labor to maintain and service the infrastructure, electricity and cooling costs, and physical security.

What makes cloud IaaS a service is paying a monthly fee to procure infrastructure instead of paying the upfront cost to build a data center and the equipment that goes in it. The cloud allows you to transition from a capitalization cost model to a utilization model in which you only pay for what you consume. The cloud data center provisions the equipment you need, and in minutes you can be up and running, using the infrastructure you have ordered. The cost of supplying the equipment to your specifications is included in your price.

The utilization model is not new, and it's the same way you purchase utilities in your home or office. Think for a second about how you are charged for electricity: You have a meter that measures how much electricity you use, and your cost is the consumption multiplied by the rate. Do you worry about the generator supplying the electricity, the building or fuel they need to operate, or even if the equipment needs maintenance? With the utilization model, you outsource these costs and to someone else and just pay for what you consume.

For example, let's imagine you purchase a powerful server with 32 processors and 128 Gigs of RAM. You would pay more to operate that server per hour than a smaller server with two processors and 1 Gig of RAM. If you decide to go on vacation and shut your infrastructure down, you stop paying the server's costs. Doesn't this sound like the same way you pay for utilities? You pay only for what you use and how much you use. IaaS allows you to forego all the high upfront costs you need to establish your system and only pay for regular monthly consumption costs.

People make a common mistake when they look at a server's cost and compare it to buying a server, and they conclude it is more cost-effective to buy the equipment. Below is an example of a small server under IAAS.

Example:

Server: Configuration: 2 CPU 4 GB memory
Cost per hour: $0.464 per hour
Cost to Run a Server:
Hours in year 365 x 24 = 8,760
Total Year Cost = $4,064.64

While it may appear cheaper to buy the equipment rather than the service, you have to remember you are only looking at the cost of purchasing the server. In this example, the Cloud provider includes in their costs the electricity to power and cool the server, the physical building to house the server, and the labor to patch the servers. You also never have to plan or fund to replace the server in 3 or 5 years when it reaches the end of its life; the price you pay includes all those factors.

Another critical factor to remember is you only pay when the server is being used. So if you want to save money, you can do so by reducing the operating hours. Shutting the server down after work hours or on the weekends, and you can cut your cost between 50% and 70%! That is the beauty of working in the cloud - you only pay for what you use.

IaaS also has many advantages when you consider your storage needs. If you need more storage space for a significant legal case, you simply purchase more, and it will instantly get provisioned to your account. You do not have to buy the equipment, install and configure it, and then power the drives. You also don't have to string cables, configure networking services, or monitor the access from a security perspective. Installation, configuration is baked into the IaaS price.

When do you use IaaS:

IaaS is needed when you need to run applications that are unique to your environment. Applications that are "homegrown" or developed in-house are great candidates for IaaS because you know the type of infrastructure needed for them to operate correctly. By having complete control of the infrastructure, you can determine where the equipment should reside, how powerful the servers need to be, and what type of contingency plans you want to put in place if you experience a problem. As you will see from the other cloud types (PaaS and SaaS), you trade off on what makes your business applications unique and your control over their design when using these different cloud models.

PaaS - Platform as a Service

Do you run a commercial software package or database in-house? Does your business depend on a standard application uniquely configured for your business? These are just two examples where PaaS could benefit your business. When you use a standard software package uniquely configured to your law firm, like a customer relationship management tool, email system, or a web server, you should consider using PaaS.

With PaaS, you can buy from a cloud provider a service that bundles the application and hardware together for a single per hour price. The advantage of doing this is you have full control over your data and applications but no longer have to meet the application's software patching and hardware management requirements. The cloud provider will upgrade your software when a new version is released. When security patches become available, it's the cloud service provider's responsibility to load them.

Below is an example of the cost to run three popular PaaS solutions:

Oracle Database	$0.06 per hour
WordPress	$0.012 per hour
Sharepoint 2016	$2.95 per hour

PaaS is also a great solution when there are intellectual property concerns over where your data needs to reside or in situations where you need to segregate and protect data from other users. Concerns over Data Security, where you need to manage who has access to data, are best addressed when running your own version of an application. PaaS can also ensure your case information or data cannot be illegally accessed by a competitor when using SaaS.

When do you use PaaS?

You should use PaaS whenever you run a standard application that has been uniquely configured for your business. Email systems, Websites, or corporate databases are all great candidates for PaaS because you get the reliability of a managed service and the extra security that comes from running your own application. Because PaaS bundles licensing costs into the service price, you may be able to reduce your licensing costs.

Other reasons to run a PaaS are reduced overall costs as technology refreshes for the hardware, patching, and power/cooling costs are included in the price. Leveraging PaaS makes an excellent decision when you want to transfer the costs and management of some management functions to your cloud provider and away from your company's technical staff. Just like with IaaS, you do not have the added expense of providing your servers with electricity, network infrastructure, or data center security.

SaaS - Software as a Service

With software as a service, you transfer more responsibility for managing your system to a cloud provider in exchange for speed in deploying your application. SaaS does this by sharing application hardware and software across multiple customers. You sacrifice some ability to customize a solution when you use SaaS, but the cost savings are substantial.

With SaaS, you are subscribing to a service through the internet for a monthly fee (sometimes there is no fee). You are purchasing software as a service and have no input to the hardware it runs on or where it operates. These offerings are very feature-rich, but their ability to customize is limited. You agree to a product and accept its features with all their benefits and limitations. If you have ever used a free web-based email account, you have experience using SaaS!

You need to be aware that you have no control over your data's security when using SaaS. It may not be encrypted or even stored in the same country as the users who depend on it. The information you enter into the system is stored in the same data repositories as other customers' data. The ability to see your data is based on the security controls the company implements. You are merely paying for a service and have no say in how the company manages its security or the hardware used to run the applications. Some factors you need to consider when using SaaS include:

Security of data in transit: Is your data encrypted as it leaves your machines and travels across the internet to the service? Look at the browser URL and see if it contains the HTTPS: syntax to know your data is encrypted as it travels from your machine to the server. Depending on the type of data transmitted, you may have concerns about keeping it secured. In some cases, you may need to prove to your customers that you are protecting their information as it is transmitted. Security is vital for financial information and case files that need to be protected when traveling across the internet.

Security of Stored Data: When you save information using SaaS, do you know if the data is encrypted? Data that is encrypted requires a private password or key to read. Even if someone else could gain access to your data, they would be unable to read it without the secret password or key. Encryption is also an excellent way to make sure only authorized users can access your company's information.

Location of Stored Data: Many industries have laws regarding where companies may store data. You would not want your financial information stored on servers located in other countries where you may be unable to extract or delete the information when you are finished. It's essential to learn where your data is stored when you use SaaS.

Backup: Does the service you use backup its data to ensure nothing is lost? If you were running your own infrastructure, you could control that process. With SaaS, you need to check that your service provider is taking the proper steps to ensure your data is recoverable in the event of a disaster.

Licensing: Have you adequately licensed the service to give your company the capability it needs? Many SaaS solutions offer single and multi-user licenses. The multi-user licenses often allow many people within your firm access to the data and provide for training and support. When selecting a SaaS product, make sure you choose the correct option at the beginning of your subscription, as it could impact your ability to configure the service.

Identity Access: Along with licenses, you need to determine the identity of people who will be using the SaaS solution and what roles or responsibilities they need. If you implement SaaS by sharing accounts, you may not only be violating the license agreement, but you will prevent your ability to know through a log file who changed the contents of a file. Identity access also gives you the power to grant and revoke access to the system at different levels. Access logs are critical when you need to prove to your customers that their information has been protected and secure.

Integration with Other Products: Using SaaS is like living on an island designed to perform a single function. Often, you need to build bridges that connect your island to other islands that perform different functions. Building bridges to transfer data is called integration, and it's critical to improving the quality of your data and making it reusable. An example of integration would be combining your payment system with your customer management software. Without integrating the systems, you will be forced to re-enter data to track customer addresses and payment information. Even worse, when the data changes, you need to go into several systems to update the account information! Many SaaS have addressed this problem by expanding their applications' functionality, but often you get a product strong in one area and sub-average in another. Integration between two robust applications will allow you to leverage the features of multiple applications.

Ability To Extract Your Data For Other Purposes: Your data belong to you, so will you have the ability to extract it from the system and use it for other purposes? There may be situations where you want to pull your client list to send holiday cards or corporate newsletters. You may wish to extract case information to analyze your workload and determine how long it takes to process a particular type of case. It is crucial when selecting a SaaS company to understand its policies around data extraction. You also want to guard against "Vendor Lock-In" if you want to switch products in the future.

Corporate Health: Knowing the corporate health of your SaaS is a complicated thing to understand. When you purchase a SaaS solution, you are committing to a company with your time and money. Do not forget with many services you pay per month, which is the extent of your relationship with that company. How would you feel after adopting a service to learn your company has been bought and now you must migrate your information to its new platform? Or what if the company simply goes out of business or plans to merge with another non-US company and tells you that you have 30 days to extract your data? Companies change their business models all the time, and you need to protect against that activity happening to you.

Most SaaS companies are privately held, and they do not have to disclose financial information to stockholders. Other companies start small and grow by offering their product at a really low cost. Their business model is not to make money on their SaaS, but rather to grow the company and sell it to a competitor. The best way to ensure that this type of activity does not impact you is to look at the SaaS company's corporate history. How long have they been in the market, and how committed are they to their customers? Free training, user conferences, and market outreach are signs that the SaaS company is committed to its customers and plans to be around a long time to serve you as their customer.

When do you use SaaS?

Software as a service is a great and economical way to perform business functions, especially for a small firm with limited time and money. Nothing prevents you from starting with a SaaS solution and upgrading to a PaaS or IaaS if your requirements change. SaaS gets you in the door and uses tools that you could never afford if you had to buy hardware and staff a data center. SaaS has helped to level the playing field among businesses, giving companies the ability to automate at low costs.

Trade-Offs

Hopefully, by now, you see the advantages of IaaS, PaaS, and SaaS. Each option has advantages and disadvantages. The choice that is best for you depends on your requirements and technical abilities. Let us face facts; you are in business to run a law firm, not run computer applications to support your business. Playing to your strengths and leveraging what you do best is an important business decision. When you decide on a cloud model, you need to factor in the technological costs for qualified staff, data center space, and people to manage licensing and security audits. There are advantages to hosting your applications, but you assume all the risks of managing the system when you do.

The simple graph below illustrates the relationship between cost and time to deployment of a computer system.

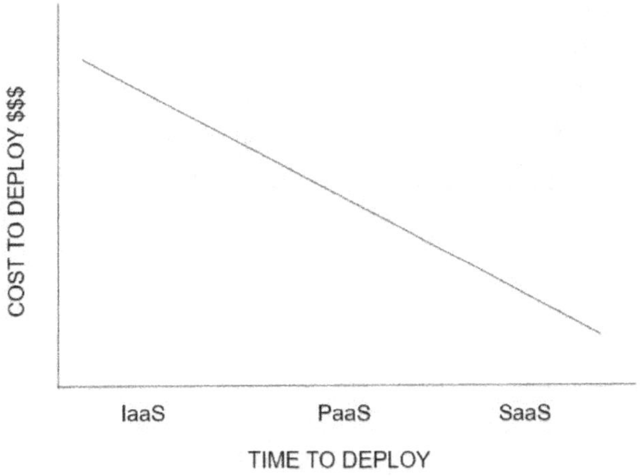

SaaS allows you to have access to a service simply by subscribing to a service. There is no need to purchase hardware and install/configure the software. You can be running in minutes using a cookie-cutter approach to a solution. As we described above, with SaaS, you use an application that limits your ability to customize and configure to your business needs.

Another way to look at the decision is to examine the internal skill set of your law firm. In the pyramid below, there are three layers. The top layer represents software as a service and its design around the skill set that only end-users will be using the system. These people do not understand the technical workings of computer software, but they know the functions they need the application to perform. They are also the people who are using the software daily and are most impacted by their functionality. Their ability to perform their job efficiently affects the financial health of the firm through their productivity. Providing this group with the ability to manage the software's configuration and settings means you do not have to hire other people to assist them. There are many advantages to using software with a large user community who have tested and provided feedback to the application developers.

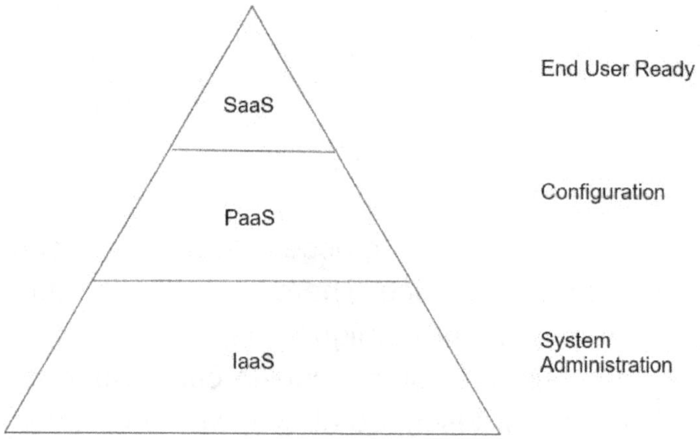

The second layer in the diagram represents Platform as a Service, and it requires the knowledge to configure the software to how a company operates. At this level, you are running and managing your customized version of an application in your data center. You will need to hire people skilled with the ability to configure the application to your needs. Examples of what makes your environment unique include unique content, workflows, licensing and performance monitoring, and account management. You will also need to manage user accounts with access to the system and the security associated with password management. As a law firm, you will need to have these people on staff, or on retainer, to provide you with the services you need within an acceptable service level agreement. At this level, your firm takes on more responsibility and accepts more risk for the application's successful management.

The last level in the diagram is system administration, and it represents IaaS. Operating at this level requires many knowledgeable people to manage a system effectively. To build a system at the Iaas level, you need to have system administration, software developers, and performance engineers on your team. You will need to manage the installation of every application as a full project and assign a project manager to the effort. In many cases, you need to purchase multiple software packages and integrate them. One example is a case management system, which may require you to buy an application server and database server to operate. The timeline to develop your system using IaaS will depend on your team's knowledge, experience with the software, and how well they know the cloud service provider.

You will need network engineers and security professionals to ensure the users can securely access the system, once it is ready for the user community. Depending on the software, you may have to establish multiple application environments to develop and test new features. You will also have to monitor the system for growth and anticipate when you need more storage or faster servers. With IaaS, you must also manage the system's security and review the logs the application generates.

The advantage of working at this level is that you get to develop your secret sauce into how the application works. Running and managing your applications allows your firm to be unique to your customers and unique in the marketplace. Don't underestimate the value of being different from the market to your customers, but go into it understanding the costs.

Moving to the Cloud

Let's say you are a medium to a small law firm, and you have determined there are many advantages to moving to the cloud, but where do you start? Is there a progression or process you should follow on your journey into the cloud?

Every cloud migration should follow a series of steps to be successful and avoid any rework. I call these steps the maturity level to cloud adoption, and they represent phases each firm must go through if they want to operate in the cloud. Each level builds on completing the previous level. Jumping layers often involve reworking as each layer builds a firm foundation for the next layer.

MATURITY LEVELS TO CLOUD ADOPTION

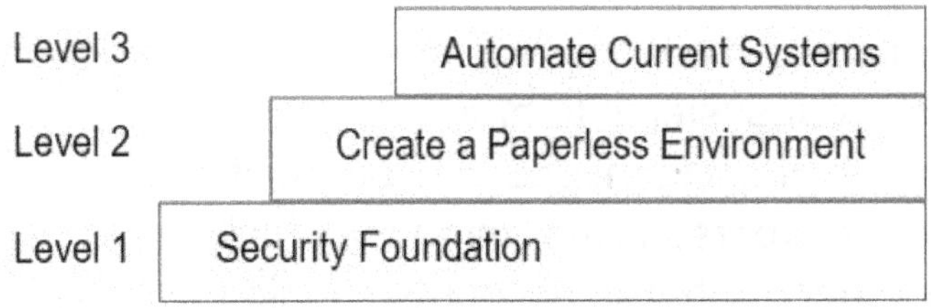

Level 1 - Security Foundation

When you operate in the cloud, you are placing your data on someone else's computer. Working in this environment is the equivalent of putting your client and corporate records in the office of another company.

Would you be willing to put physical files in someone else's office without ensuring that information is protected? What policies and procedures do you need to have in place to protect your client's data from computer hackers and other companies who want to access the information illegally?

Building on a security foundation means you develop the ability to trace access to data back to an individual and, most importantly, identify unauthorized access to data records. The same controls you develop in real life also need to be implemented in the cloud. In a cloud, security must be the focal point in everything you do, and it all starts with identity management. In the same way you would have a process and procedure to give someone keys to a physical file room you need to think about what needs to be in place before giving someone electronic access.

Identity management requires each person who accesses your systems to have a unique name and password. If an incident occurs, you must have the ability to link it to the person who made the change during the security breach. Shared accounts should never be allowed. You should have policies that express to your employees that password management is as important to your organization as a physical key the office would be. You need to enforce strong password management, which means a password length of at least eight characters and a mixture of letters, numbers, and special symbols. Also, having the same password for every system is not the right answer, as a breach to one system means all your accounts are compromised. The only acceptable password policy is making sure each application has a unique and complex password. Fortunately, there are many useful password management tools available that make this function easy to manage.

You must not underestimate the value of enabling two-factor authentication for your applications. While it can be a nuisance to provide a second password, it makes access to your cloud-based even more difficult for those who would do you harm. Follow adequate security procedures for all accounts associated with your business because any security breach will impact your company's credibility.

Finally, do not treat your social media accounts, email, and website accounts any differently than your bank account or client files. These accounts need to be locked down and protected because they depict what people see when they think of you and represent your reputation. Think about the damage that can be done to your reputation if malicious emails are generated from your corporate email account. Would your clients trust that their records are safely protected if they know you can't protect your email or social media accounts? What if a competitor was able to alter your corporate website and change its content?

Level 2 - Create a Paperless Environment

Think of paper as an anchor which ties you down to a physical location. With paper, you need to manage and secure its location, and most importantly, store the physical copies. Maintaining paper is also expensive when you think about the time it takes to access your files and file them appropriately. A lost paper file could mean the difference in how a legal case is handled and reflects poorly on your practice. Add to the handling cost the real estate expense you pay for the square footage to store file cabinets!

Going paperless means that every document you touch is scanned and stored electronically. The upfront investment in scanning a document yields many advantages over physical files, besides being able to retrieve the document on your computer. By moving to a paperless environment, you can:

> **Improve Accessibility to Your Files:** You can retrieve your files anyplace at any time, across the internet. Gone are the days of having to take the correct physical files home or on a trip. It will also allow you access to your notes, procedures, and templates.
>
> **Reduce Storage Costs:** Say good-bye to file boxes and file cabinets. With a paperless environment, you no longer need to reserve physical space to maintain your files. Storage costs can be considerable when you factor in the physical space to keep paper files. The costs of

physical storage and refiling documents go away, allowing you to use your time more effectively.

Ability to Share: With electronic files, you can share case information with other people or companies by either making an electronic copy of the file or permitting access to your files. Gone are the costs associated with copying and shipping physical paper.

Search Capabilities: Have you ever needed to search through hundreds of pages to reference a particular person or company? If you store your files electronically, you can pass that task off to your computer, which, depending on the program you use, can search many file types, including PDFs. Electronic searching is much more useful than conducting the search yourself or hiring an assistant. Search capabilities also allow you to explore documents in less time and with a higher accuracy level.

Organization: Paper files' movement requires good organizational skills to make sure nothing is lost or becomes separated from its case. When you store files electronically, they are always in the directory you place them. Setting up your on-line file system is an investment that yields many benefits when you need to locate information. How you organize your electronic files can be very involved with folders and subfolders to identify information, or you can have a single folder per case. The complexity of the cases you work on will determine which folder structure works best for you.

Track Access: Have you ever lost a file or do not know who had taken it? With the move to a paperless environment, you no longer must worry, because the document will always be in the same location. You can use document management software that can log when the file was accessed and by whom. Most systems can even tell you what changes were made in the file. The level of access you deploy will depend on your firm's size and attorneys' number in your practice.

Moving to a paperless environment involves a commitment to scanning and storing every paper document you retrieve. With the right type of scanner and filing system, the process can become routine and fast. Many copiers, or office printers, can scan single and double sides of a paper very quickly. If you handle a lot of paper, a dedicated scanner may be required. There are many ways to move towards a paperless office, but the key is you need to be committed to working with electronic documents and stick with it. If you decide to keep a hybrid of physical and electronic records in a case, you will end up with a hybrid filing system. Scan and electronically store everything, and you will reap the many benefits of being a paperless office.

Level 3 - Automate Current Business Processes

As a law practice grows and starts to handle multiple clients, the internal business process starts to develop. You quickly learn what information you need to gather from your client, you create methods for tracking your time, and you develop a system for monitoring tasks associated with the case. These processes evolve because they save you time and help you deliver better results for your clients.

Every time you repeat a business process, you are developing an internal business process unique to your company and a process that you should consider automating. Your business processes are what makes your company unique and special. The business processes you produce distinguishes you and your firm from your competitors.

When you are a solo practitioner, the business process can be informal because only you need to know the steps required to achieve the outcome you want. As your firm grows and you handle multiple cases, your time becomes more limited. You may need to delegate some of your business processes to others or find new ways to complete these vital tasks. Without a documented process, the quality of work can vary based on which person in the firm performs the business process. Tasks that are infrequently performed may require extra time as you have to relearn your business process.

If this problem sounds familiar, you need to take the next step and document your business processes. By formalizing the steps, you enable the business process to be conducted the same way each time, regardless of who performs the work. Documentation also allows you to delegate work that you do not want to do. Did you become a lawyer because you wanted to manage your billing process, market your services, or calculate your taxes? You became a lawyer because you want to help people find legal solutions to their problems and fight injustice. Supporting tasks such as marketing are important to the success of your firm, but they do not have to be done by you personally.

Fortunately, many of the business processes you need to develop can be automated using SaaS. As you see later in this book, SaaS solutions have been developed for many business needs and can be configured to match your unique processes. An added advantage is many of these solutions will provide your clients with 24x7x365 access to your services. Another advantage of using cloud software is that you only pay a monthly fee for the service. Imagine getting access to thousands of software development hours needed to create a product for just a few dollars per month!

Cloud-Based Software Solutions

In the previous chapters, we defined the cloud and the different types of cloud services. This chapter will look at other SaaS products that are available to simplify and improve your legal practice. The following pages group applications by business functions that every law firm performed in their daily business. You will find several programs listed under categories, along with a summary and information about features, security, and cost. This list is not a complete list of applications, as new companies enter, merge, or leave the marketplace all the time. Consider these options as a starting point in finding the applications that are the best fit for your business.

Which application is the best for your business depends on your requirements. How willing are you to adjust your business process to match the program, and how much money you are ready to spend? In deciding, you should conduct due diligence by reviewing websites, watching YouTube videos, and getting references from your peers. Take advantage of the free trials that many of these companies offer, but only use dummy data until you decide. You don't want to have your client or business information left on a system you will not use. By testing with dummy data, you can experiment with many scenarios and not have any business impact.

The beauty and frustration about working in the cloud are that change is constant. The features that don't exist today could be present in the next release, or new vendors can pop up with innovative solutions. Companies offering different solutions could also merge, allowing a single vendor to serve you in multiple ways. Keep an open mind to change and re-evaluate every year if the decisions you made when you started are still the right ones for your firm.

Keep in mind that your decisions do not prevent you from changing to new applications in the future. Most companies charge a monthly fee, and many offer discounts for paying for a whole year upfront. Your software investment is minimal in comparison to supporting the infrastructure it was running on. Your most significant investment is in the time it would take to migrate to a new system, if that becomes your decision.

Reviewing the information provided on each system in the following pages will help you make the best decision for your firm. Your choices on which application to use should be based on your current business requirements. Carefully consider the type of licenses you will need and your security requirements when making your decision.

Requirement Definition

How do you go about defining your requirements so fancy videos and websites do not sway you? After reviewing several options in a category, my suggestion is to go back and specify your needs on paper and then rate each application against it.

Example: Appointment Applications:

Business features:

- *Schedule appointments 24 x7*
- *Access through a smartphone*
- *Block out time when clients cannot make appointments*
- *Allow the ability to schedule recurring events*
- *Ability to send out a cancellation notice*
- *Ability to reach customers through text messages*
- *Bilingual support*
- *Customization with business logo/name*
- *Interaction with the internal calendar system*
- *Ability to report on appointments by client*
- *Ability to track missed appointments*

Platform:

- *Windows*
- *iOS*
- *Android*
- *Mobile devices*

Security:

- *Two Factor Authentication*
- *Backup*
- *Identity management*
- *Encryption of data in storage*
- *Encryption of data during transmission*

Cost:

- *Single User Cost*
- *Multi-User Cost*

Only you can define the business features which are essential to you. Some features may be “required” which other components are “nice to have.” You can always skip a “nice to have” requirement, but the solution you pick must address all your “required” business features. Do your research, and don’t be afraid to reach out to the vendor to get your questions answered or request a demonstration. The time you spend researching is an investment that will pay dividends later when the product you select functions correctly.

Factors to Consider

Cost: Each cloud-based solution deploys a different pricing model. The model can be as simple as the number of users per month, or features can be bundled into product offerings. The key is to have a good understanding of what you need and realize that you can always upgrade in the future if your requirements change.

Almost all cloud-based solutions offer a free trial for you to explore their solution. Take advantage of the offering and experiment with the application before making a decision. You may find the user interface of one solution more appealing than the other or understand its workflow better. Another factor to consider is how does each solution produce the reports or documentation your clients will receive.

Many cloud-based solutions will offer you a discount for paying for the entire year’s cost upfront as it guarantees them revenue and locks you into their solution. While the cost savings may be attractive, only consider doing this if you are convinced the product meets your needs. You can always start month to month and then switch to an annual payment later, after gaining experience using the tool.

Do not forget the advantage of working in the cloud is you can buy what you need. You should be prepared to adjust your licensing to meet your needs. Be prepared to add and subtract per user licenses as your staffing levels change. Avoid prepaying for the entire year to get a discount until you have a steady staffing level and adjust your licensing monthly to achieve more significant cost savings.

Platform Availability: How will you access the application? Most cloud-based solutions will work from any desktop (Mac or Windows) without a problem when using an internet browser. But, as you will see, many services also offer a mobile-based application to work on your smartphone or mobile device. If you use one type of mobile device/smartphone, pay careful attention to the offering. Selecting a product incompatible with your smartphone will tie you to your desk and impact your productivity. Switching mobile devices/smartphones may not be an option based on your wireless plan.

Security

2 Factor Authentication: In the previous section, the advantage of moving to 2-factor authentication was discussed. Many software applications offer 2-factor authentication, and you should always try to choose a product that utilizes it, as it shows the company's commitment to security and protecting your data. Remember, 2-factor security only protects you if you enable it!

Data Security: There are two types of data security you should consider when selecting a cloud-based application solution. How is your data protected at rest (storage) and transit (traveling through the internet)? In both cases, you want to make sure encryption is used, and you want to make sure the type of encryption is at least 256 bit or utilizes Advanced Encryption Standard (AES).

Data encrypted at storage means the data stored on the application's server is encrypted. This encryption type will protect you from system administrators, other customers of the applications, and hackers, any of whom may gain access to your data. If they could access your data, they would need to have your encryption key to decode and read the information. Since you have no control over how or where your data is stored, knowing that it is encrypted should be a requirement when selecting a solution.

Data encrypted in transit means that as your data travels through the internet, the data is encrypted to prevent it from being read by anyone who does not contain the encryption key. The scary reality of the internet is there is no single owner. Your data can take multiple routes to reach you from the service provider. If one circuit along the path fails, the internet is resilient enough to send your data to a different route. Each time your data gets routed, it can be captured. Encryption in transit is essential when dealing with sensitive client data that you need to protect. You know your data is encrypted if you see an HTTPS: link in the URL bar or a padlock icon in the browser.

GDRP stands for General Data Protection Regulation. The GDRP is a security standard implemented by European Union Law on May 25, 2018, and addresses the rights consumers have when providing personal data to a company. It also spells out how the company will use, share, and erase the data when it is no longer needed. GDRP is a requirement for all companies operating in the European Union, but many US companies follow these standards voluntarily. Knowing that a company follows GDRP demonstrates they understand data sensitivity and the need to protect personal data.

Data Center: When a company states that their data center is certified as SOC2 Type II, they are stating an internal audit of their system safeguards has been conducted. Performed by an independent third party, SOC audits identify security weaknesses a company needs to address. The controls deal with physical access to the data center, backup power, network capabilities, server patching, etc. When a company states they are SOC 2 Type II compliant, it does not mean they are doing everything correctly. It means the company has had an audit to identify its strengths and weaknesses. Selecting a solution that has undergone a SOC 2 Type II audit tells you the company values security and is committed to improving it at all levels.

Other Factors

Integration: Remember that even while your data lives on someone else's server, it is still your data. There will be cases where you need to extract your data for other uses, and knowing that you can extract your data is an essential consideration in selecting a software package. Many applications are designed to interact with other applications, which will make your job easier. Knowing that your case management application can integrate with a mail management program will make your job easier if you want to send your clients a newsletter for a birthday greeting. Look for applications that allow for integration.

Training: Having the most sophisticated program is meaningless if you don't know how to use it correctly. Many companies offer free training sessions to onboard new users, and others rely on third-party trainers. The amount of training available for a cloud-based solution will vary based on the complexity of the program and the breadth of its user base. Select a cloud-based solution that provides you with training based on how you like to learn.

Inventory of Cloud-Based Applications

-

APPOINTMENT MANAGEMENT

Acuity Scheduling

OVERVIEW:
Acuity helps business owners take control of their time, and more importantly, their calendars. The application provides appointment booking directly through a website using Acuity online appointment scheduling software. Clients can schedule their appointments online, provide information to the business through forms, and pay for services with a credit card online.

The application also eliminates no-show appointments through the use of automatic text messages and email reminders to clients. The scheduling page provides clients the ability to book appointments from their desktop, tablet, or phone. Business owners are also able to manage appointments directly. Some of the features included in this program include:

- Calendar Sync
- Online Credit Card payments
- Sell gift certificates, packages, memberships, or group classes
- Integrated with video conferencing programs
- Sends reminder emails and texts to customers
- Customization to your brand

WEBSITE: https://www.acuityscheduling.com/
FEATURE:
https://www.acuityscheduling.com/signup.php?var=acuity-2

Acuity Scheduling

SOFTWARE COST

Free Trial Offer:	Yes - 7 days
Subscription:	Monthly and Yearly
Price:	$14 per month 1 user $23 per month 6 users $45 per month 36 users

AVAILABLE ON

Platform:	Browser-based
	Mobile
	iOS

SECURITY

2 Factor Authentication:	Unknown
Data Security:	Complies with GDRP
Data Center:	Certified SOC2 Type II

Other Features

Integration:	Square Zapier Stripe PayPal
Training:	Web-based training Webinars

AppointmentPlus

OVERVIEW:

Designed with a focus on medium to small businesses, AppointmentPlus has many features that will save you time. The application allows clients to select a time you mark as available, send appointment reminders by email and text messages, handle payment, and integrate with your website or Facebook account. You can set up multiple appointments per time slot, manage conference room allocations which are all features necessary for larger firms.

Large businesses can use analytical reporting tools, add extra fields to capture client-specific information, and create scheduling templates for services that require repeat visits. Your customers will have the ability to book appointments 24/7/365 from their computer or mobile device. AppointmentPlus reduces the time and effort needed to schedule appointments, allowing you to spend more time with your customers.

WEBSITE: https://www.appointmentplus.com/

FEATURE: https://www.appointmentplus.com/pricing/

AppointmentPlus

SOFTWARE COST

Free Trial Offer:	No
Subscription:	Monthly and Yearly
Price:	Basic features start at $49 per month Platinum features start at $199 per month

AVAILABLE ON

Platform:	Browser-based
	Mobile
	iOS

SECURITY

2 Factor Authentication:	Unknown
Data Security:	Data encrypted in transit
Data Center:	Unknown

Other Features

Integration:	Yes
Training:	

CASE MANAGEMENT

Caselines

OVERVIEW:

Purchased by Thomson Reuters in 2020, CaseLines helps you manage documents associated with a legal case by storing them in the cloud. Once the documents are stored and security permissions set, you can add notes, cross-link documents, and share documents with other parties. The power of Caselines is its ability to be used in court, giving all parties in the room the same shared view across multiple monitors.

Caselines' unique bundling and paging framework allows all parties to stay in sync when reviewing or referencing case documents. The document owner controls permissions, and costs are tied to the volume of information stored. The three primary functions of Caselines are:

- Building Case Bundles
- Collaboration and Review
- Court Presentation

WEBSITE: http://caselines.com/
FEATURES:
Bundling: https://caselines.com/product/bundle-building
Court Presentation:
https://caselines.com/product/court-presentation

CASELINE

COST

Free Trial Offer:	
Subscription:	
Price:	Based on volume - Need to contact

AVAILABLE ON

Platform:	Browser-based

SECURITY

2 Factor Authentication:	Unknown
Data Security:	GDRP California Consumer Privacy Act of 2018
Data Center:	Unknown

Other Features

Integration:	
Training:	Yes

CLIO

OVERVIEW:

CLIO is a comprehensive suite of products that integrates customer and case management tools to manage a legal practice. It allows you to track your client's information, provide online payment features, and generate reports. CLIO manages the documents in your cases through bundling documents and provides the ability to annotate documents with notes. The tool's built-in marketing features allow you to enhance your client relationship by using intake forms, emails, and customer reminders.

The flexibility of CLIO is its ability to support small to large firms using its products. The price you pay is based on the number of users and the features you need, so the product can grow as your needs expand. This product handles the day administrative tasks for attorneys through features such as time tracking, billing, matter management, full-text search, court calendaring, and e-signatures. Access to information is also available through a dashboard and integration to other tools like Microsoft Office and Quickbooks on-line.

WEBSITE: https://www.clio.com/
FEATURES: https://www.clio.com/pricing/

CLIO

COST

Free Trial Offer:	Yes
Subscription:	Yes
Price:	Starting at $39 per month

AVAILABLE ON

Platform:	Browser-based
	Mobile
	iOS

SECURITY

2 Factor Authentication:	Yes
Data Security:	GDRP
Data Center:	SOC 2

Other Features

Integration:	Yes
Training:	Yes

CosmoLex

OVERVIEW:

Cosmolex is a tool built specifically for law firms. It integrates billing, practice management, and accounting into one solution, so you have all the information you need to run your law practice in one place. For one price you get under one account the following essential business functions:

- Calendar and Task Management
- Business Accounting
- Legal Time and Billing
- Accounting
- Document and Email Integration
- Secure Client Portal

One-click billing allows you to generate an invoice that summarizes all the time spent working on a case and any additional expenses. Overdue reminders can be sent automatically to your clients, eliminating the need to chase down payments. CosmoLex even can handle trust disbursements and 3rd party lien claims. All transactions are recorded in the accounting system and allow for three-way reconciliation between your books, your bank balance, and your company ledger. CosmoLex helps your legal practice stay efficient and customer-focused.

WEBSITE: https://www.cosmolex.com/
FEATURES: https://www.cosmolex.com/pricing/

CosmoLex

COST

Free Trial Offer:	Yes
Subscription:	Yes
Price:	$79 per user per month for a yearly subscription

AVAILABLE ON

Platform:	Windows
	iOS

SECURITY

2 Factor Authentication:	Yes
Data Security:	
Data Center:	

Other Features

Integration:	Yes
Training:	Yes

Keap

OVERVIEW:

Keap is a Customer Relationship Management (CRM) suite of applications designed to help a small business grow. They offer three integrated products designed to improve your business processes.

> Keap Grow: Designed to help startups and new business be more efficient in responding to client needs
>
> Keap Pro: Includes Keap Grow features and allows you to develop repeatable sales processes and marketing campaigns.
>
> Infusionsoft: Robust CRM product that allows you to manage your customer while marketing to grow your business.

Through the consolidation of contact information, Keap's CRM products improve your sales process by eliminating redundant activities and empowering e-commerce tools. Tap into new leads by fully utilizing email, social media, and offline channels to build relationships through keap.

WEBSITE: https://keap.com/
FEATURES: https://keap.com/pricing

Keap

COST

Free Trial Offer:	Yes
Subscription:	Yes
Price:	$56 up to $140 per month depending on features

AVAILABLE ON

Platform:	Browser-based

SECURITY

2 Factor Authentication:	Yes
Data Security:	Yes
Data Center:	SOC 2 Type II

Other Features

Integration:	Yes
Training:	Yes

PracticePanther

OVERVIEW:

PracticePanther is a law practice management suite designed for law firms. Its three areas of focus are the management of cases, invoices, and clients:

Case Management: Provides you with access to everything you need to know about your client's case via a smartphone, tablet, notebook, or desktop computer. Track documents, emails, and contact information related to your clients all in one place. Gather information from your customer using intake forms, and use workflow to track each step of the process.

Invoice Management: A built-in time and expense tracking application allows you to correctly invoice your clients for their time working on their case. You can generate invoices from the system and track the payment.

Client Management: PracticePanter has a customer relationship manager's features to help you build and manage the relationship you have established with your clients. Use intake forms to collect customer information, schedule meeting, share documents, and have the system generate emails and text reminders.

WEBSITE: https://www.practicepanther.com/
FEATURES: https://www.practicepanther.com/pricing/

PracticePanther

COST

Free Trial Offer:	Yes
Subscription:	Yes
Price:	The solo package is $39 per user per month The business package is $79 per user per month

AVAILABLE ON

Platform:	Browser-based
	Android
	iOS

SECURITY

2 Factor Authentication:	Yes
Data Security:	Data encrypted at rest and in transit
Data Center:	

Other Features

Integration:	Yes
Training:	Yes

Rocket Matter

OVERVIEW:

Rocket Matter is an integrated suite of tools that will help your law firm automate its business processes and saves you time to focus on your clients. The suite of tools allows you to track the steps in your case by building templates and workflows, securely collects payments from your clients, and generate reports to help you track the status of multiple cases. Rocket Matter also provides your firm with a customer portal that allows for the safe management of documents and provides your customer with the case's status, upcoming court dates, and payment information. The portal gives your clients access to their case information 24/7/365.

Some of the many features included are:

- Calendaring and Tasks
- Contact Management
- Reporting
- Integration to Other Tools
- Collaboration
- Robust Mobile Applications

WEBSITE: https://www.rocketmatter.com/
FEATURES:
https://www.rocketmatter.com/awesome-features/

Rocket Matter

COST

Free Trial Offer:	Yes
Subscription:	Yes
Price:	The Essential package is $25 per user per month The Pro package is $55 per user per month

AVAILABLE ON

Platform:	Browser-based
	Android
	iOS

SECURITY

2 Factor Authentication:	
Data Security:	GDRP compliant
Data Center:	

Other Features

Integration:	Yes
Training:	Yes

CHATBots

Intercom

OVERVIEW:

Intercom creates chatbots that reside on your website. Chatbots can answer the most frequently asked questions, freeing your employees for other types of work. ChatBots provide your prospective clients with the answers to basic questions, links to other pages on the site, or can gather information through on-line forms. ChatBots can listen for incoming messages and respond when it knows the correct answer, or direct the conversation to a human on your team.

Intercom Chat Bots also allow you to gather the information your company can use for marketing. You can collect statistics on the types of inquiries you receive and modify your website to address the most common types of questions, thus improving your service. You can uncover new ways to serve your customers by understanding why people are coming to your website and develop new types of services based on their input. ChatBots provide you with a 24 x 7 x 365 way to interact with your customers and build a stronger relationship.

WEBSITE: https://www.intercom.com/
FEATURES:
https://www.intercom.com/pricing?on_pageview_event=pricing_nav

Intercom

COST

Free Trial Offer:	Yes
Subscription:	Yes
Price:	Starting at $39 per month

AVAILABLE ON

Platform:	Browser-based
	Mobile
	iOS

SECURITY

2 Factor Authentication:	Yes
Data Security:	EU-US Privacy Shield
Data Center:	SCO2

Other Features

Integration:	Yes
Training:	Yes

Lawdroid

OVERVIEW:

Lawdroid offers three types of bots designed to handle administrative tasks that consume the time of many attorneys. They offer three bots:

Reception Bot: Captures website visitor information
Paralegal Bot: Gathers clients information and manage cases
LegalHealth Check Bot: Helps clients to diagnose legal issues

The bots improve your interaction with clients by providing attorneys the ability to gather information efficiently when a prospective client is at their site. By providing legal information, links to resources, and answering questions, you start to build a relationship immediately with the visitor.

The tool gives you the ability to capture the prospective client's interests and learn why people visit your website. LawDroid consultants help you build the droid based on their experience helping other customers, allowing you to benefit from their years of experience. Data can also be exported to other tools eliminating duplicative data entry.

WEBSITE: https://lawdroid.com/
FEATURES: https://lawdroid.com/bot-automation-service-for-lawyers/

Lawdroid

COST

Free Trial Offer:	
Subscription:	Yes
Price:	Rates vary based on features and the number of attorneys

AVAILABLE ON

Platform:	Browser-based

SECURITY

2 Factor Authentication:	
Data Security:	
Data Center:	

Other Features

Integration:	
Training:	

COLLABORATION

Slack

OVERVIEW:

Slack allows teams to work together using a concept called channels. Channels allow you to group information around projects, cases, departments, office locations, or any grouping of people. Within those channels, users can access a set of tools and services currently used in their business, such as emails, text messages, files, and data. Slack allows you to share your information with your team members, which eliminates duplication and increases transparency. The tool's power lies in its ability to consolidate information so you can find what you need quickly and efficiently.

Everything contained within Slack is automatically archived and indexed. Companies can automatically create a comprehensive knowledge base using the index without the need for special documentation. The tool also can create workflows that allow you to automate a business process that involves multiple people within the channel. The ability to encrypt data within the tool also exists, ensuring only the right people can see the data they need to do their job. Slack helps teams work smarter by providing all of the necessary information and context in one location.

WEBSITE: https://slack.com/
FEATURES: https://slack.com/features

Slack

COST

Free Trial Offer:	Yes
Subscription:	Yes
Price:	Free for small teams up to $12.50 for advanced features

AVAILABLE ON

Platform:	Browser-based
	Mobile
	iOS

SECURITY

2 Factor Authentication:	Yes
Data Encryption:	Yes
Data Center:	SOC 2 - Type II

Other Features

Integration:	Yes
Training:	Yes

Skype

OVERVIEW:
Skype is a video conferencing software that can make voice and video calls between one or multiple connections. It provides video chat and voice calls from computers, mobile devices, and tablets across the internet for free. Currently, Skype can connect up to 50 people in one video call session.

The power of Skype lies in its ability to integrate voice, video, and instant messaging into a single call. Users of the service are not limited in their communication methods, as Skype can merge voice and video calls into a single conversation. In addition to voice chat, video chat, and IM, Skype enables file transfers, SMS, screen-sharing, and video conferencing, making it a popular business tool. Skype is available as a mobile application on your phone or tablet and on your desktop computer, where it can run within your web browser as an extension.

Other features of Skype include the ability to transcribe and record conversations automatically. You can also call landlines directly from the Skype interface or even receive phone calls at a dedicated phone number. Skype provides a reliable and cost-effective way for businesses of any size to communicate with each other and with clients.

WEBSITE: https://skype.com
FEATURES: https://www.skype.com/en/features/

Skype

COST

Free Trial Offer:	Yes
Subscription:	No - Cost based on usage
Price:	Free but costs for calling landlines or use of calls and private numbers features

AVAILABLE ON

Platform:	Browser-based
	Mobile
	iOS

SECURITY

2 Factor Authentication:	No
Data Security:	Yes
Data Center:	

Other Features

Integration:	Yes - to MS Office Products
Training:	Yes

MS Teams

OVERVIEW:

MS Teams is a communication platform that integrates video conference calls, instant messaging, file sharing, with the ability to share a common workspace. Microsoft is phasing MS Teams in to replace Skype for Business and Microsoft Classroom.

The power of MS teams is its integration with other MS Office products. You can view and edit MS Office documents within the tool as well as access one drive. Within Teams, you can establish channels based on a project, product, or business units. The benefit of channels is the ability to share your information across the channel, eliminating data duplicity and increasing efficiency in finding information.

MS Teams also contains a video conferencing feature, which allows for integrating video and voice calls. You also can share a screen and record a meeting for playback at a later time.

WEBSITE: https://www.microsoft.com/en-us/microsoft-365/microsoft-teams/group-chat-software
FEATURES:https://www.microsoft.com/en-us/microsoft-365/microsoft-teams/compare-microsoft-teams-options

MS Teams

COST

Free Trial Offer:	Yes
Subscription:	Yes
Price:	Free to $20 user fee per month

AVAILABLE ON

Platform:	Browser-based
	Mobile
	iOS

SECURITY

2 Factor Authentication:	Yes
Data Security:	Yes
Data Center:	Yes

Other Features

Integration:	Yes
Training:	Yes

Zoom

OVERVIEW:
Zoom is a video conferencing platform that enables online meetings, webinars, and file sharing. Users can join a Zoom meeting using an internet connection or dialing into a conference bridge and entering a meeting number. The ability to integrate voice and internet calls makes it a useful tool for users who do not have access to an internet connection.

With its breakthrough tile display, Zoom can bring multiple users together in a way that still makes everyone feel part of the conversation. Another unique feature of Zoom is its ability to have breakout rooms for smaller conversations. Using this feature meeting, participants can leave the larger group for a private discussion or work out an issue; then, they rejoin the central meeting to share information.

Zoom's desktop and native mobile apps allow teams to connect and collaborate from any device. The business packages also allow you to brand the Zoom interface with your company logo, so your users will not realize they are using the tool. The business packages also allow you to have transcripts made of the conversation. Zoom can capture and record a meeting for later playback by users, making it a great training tool.

WEBSITE: https://zoom.us/
FEATURES: https://zoom.us/pricing

Zoom

TEAMS COST

Free Trial Offer:	Yes
Subscription:	Yes
Price:	Free to $250 per year for different services

AVAILABLE ON

Platform:	Browser-based
	Mobile
	iOS

SECURITY

2 Factor Authentication:	Yes
Data Security:	Yes
Data Center:	SOC2 Type 2

Other Features

Integration:	Yes
Training:	Yes

ENTERPRISE SOFTWARE

Office 365

OVERVIEW:

Microsoft Office 365 is an enterprise cloud collaboration tool that provides your office with the ability to have:

- Private and secure space to store your files
- Online access to Microsoft Outlook, Word, Excel, Powerpoint
- Online access to cloud services: Teams, Onedrive, SharePoint
- Connect dispersed teams using shared calendars
- Messaging and conferencing tools
- Emails, Instant messaging and online websites
- Voice and video calling

The advantage of using Office 365 is that all the Microsoft tools you currently use for business are integrated. Office 365 allows you to schedule an MS Teams meeting from your calendar or add your work documents stored in Onedrive directly to your email. The integration between the products saves you time as you can integrate the features of Office 365 to enhance your productivity.

WEBSITE: https://products.office.com/
FEATURES:
https://www.microsoft.com/en-us/microsoft-365/business/compare-all-microsoft-365-business-products

Office365

COST

Free Trial Offer:	Yes
Subscription:	Yes
Price:	$5 per user/month

AVAILABLE ON

Platform:	Browser-based
	Android
	iOS

SECURITY

2 Factor Authentication:	Yes
Data Security:	Yes
Data Center:	SOC 2 Type II

Other Features

Integration:	Yes
Training:	Yes

Google Workspace

OVERVIEW:

Google Workspace (formerly G-Suite) combines all the google office productivity tools into an all-in-one suite for universal access across teams. The suite contains:

- Gmail
- Calendar
- Meet / Chat
- Google Drive
- Docs / Sheets / Slides/ Forms / Sites

G-Suite administrators can add and remove users, set up groups, and add verification steps and single sign-on (SSO) from a single console. Google Workspace provides integration between all its tools to provide a complete work environment.

The advantage of using Google Workspace is that all Google products your use are integrated. You can schedule a Google Meet from your calendar or add your work documents stored directly to your email in your Google Drive. The integration between the products saves you time as you can integrate the product's features to enhance your productivity.

WEBSITE: https://workspace.google.com/
EATURES: https://workspace.google.com/pricing.html

Google Workspace

COST

Free Trial Offer:	Yes
Subscription:	Yes
Price:	Starting at $6 per month

AVAILABLE ON

Platform:	Browser-based
	Android
	iOS

SECURITY

2 Factor Authentication:	Yes
Data Security:	Yes
Data Center:	SOC 2 Type II

Other Features

Integration:	Yes
Training:	Yes

ELECTRONIC SIGNATURE

DocuSign eSignature

OVERVIEW:
DocuSign eSignature is an electronic signature solution that lets you securely sign documents with your customers. You can sign documents from Windows, iOS, and Android devices using the company's data encryption tool. DocuSign enables you to sign documents in 43 different languages.

The tool allows you to add fields to your document to record the date or document type. Using the DocuSign application, you can track your documents' status and set automatic reminders and receive notifications when the document is signed. DocuSign provides integration to 350+ applications allowing you to build workflows to external applications. You can set up workflows ranging from single-step processes to multi-party, multi-step transactions.

DocuSign's eSignatures complies with the U.S. ESIGN Act and UETA, allowing your documents to be admissible in court. The tool automatically generates and stores an audit log for every agreement so you can vouch for who has accessed and signed the document.

WEBSITE:
https://www.docusign.com/products/electronic-signature
FEATURES:https://www.docusign.com/products-and-pricing

DocuSign eSignature

COST

Free Trial Offer:	Yes
Subscription:	Yes
Price:	$10 per month

AVAILABLE ON

Platform:	Browser-based
	Android
	iOS
	Windows

SECURITY

2 Factor Authentication:	Yes
Data Security:	
Data Center:	

Other Features

Integration:	Yes
Training:	Yes

SignNow

OVERVIEW
SignNow is a cloud-based electronic signature solution that allows businesses to capture legally-binding signatures. You can capture signatures across various documents through any device and the platform (single and multi-party). SignNow also offers cloud storage integrations, authentication tools, customizable branding, and shared templates. Advanced options allow users to designate required fields, pre-fill documents with text, utilize field validators to ensure the information provided is valid, and add labels giving the document recipient instructions.

To alert users to the need for signatures, SignNow allows you to create custom signing invitations to be sent to recipients. You also can send bulk invites to multiple recipients, define signing orders, and set expiration dates on document signing links. Users also can request supplementary information from signers through the use of required fields and set reminders for unsigned documents. SignNow even can send you a notification when the document is signed. Signers can also decline to sign documents and change their minds later on, with an automatic reminder delivered to the recipient 24 hours after signing.

WEBSITE: https://www.signnow.com/
FEATURES:https://snseats.signnow.com/purchase/business_plans/pricing?from=signnow

SignNow

COST

Free Trial Offer:	Yes
Subscription:	Yes
Price:	$8 per user per month $30 per user per month for 10 online users

AVAILABLE ON

Platform:	Browser-based
	Android
	iOS

SECURITY

2 Factor Authentication:	Yes
Data Security:	Encryption at rest and transit
Data Center:	Soc 2 Type 2

Other Features

Integration:	Yes
Training:	

FILE STORAGE

Box

OVERVIEW:

Box is a cloud storage solution that allows users to store, manage, and share files inside your organization and securely with people outside your firm. The service provides you with 100 GB of storage in the lowest plan and unlimited storage for just $35 per month per user. Box includes built-in integration to other products like Office 365 and Google Workplace, making the service easy to use.

Using Box, you can control permissions on your files, custom brand your file storage site, and set password policies for users who want to access the files you wish to share. Box also allows you to automate workflow processes so that documents can move between users automatically based on actions taken. Workflows allow you to focus on the work that needs to be done and not on finding the document.

Box can also integrate with other applications, through its extensive library of interfaces. The ability to reference documents in Box from other applications helps simplify your work environment and maintains a unified content experience.

WEBSITE: https://www.box.com/
FEATURES: https://www.box.com/pricing

Box

COST

Free Trial Offer:	Yes
Subscription:	Yes
Price:	$5 per user/month starting

AVAILABLE ON

Platform:	Browser-based
	Android
	iOS

SECURITY

2 Factor Authentication:	Yes
Data Security:	FIPS 140-2
Data Center:	SOC 2 Type II

Other Features

Integration:	Yes
Training:	Yes

Dropbox

OVERVIEW:

Dropbox is a cloud-based file-sharing application that allows you to bring all your team's content together into one location. Dropbox can be used to back up your computer, maintain version history for 30 days, smart sync with your desktop files, and provides full-text search.

In the team's version, you can manage files by groups, integrate with other applications using API, and establish tier administrative roles. Dropbox also maintains extensive log files that can show you who and when an individual file was last accessed. The individual plan states at $19/99 per month per user and includes 3 TB of secure storage. The advanced package includes unlimited storage at $25 per month per user.

Dropbox has a strong focus on security, allowing administrators to encrypt data storage and its transmission using 256-bit AES and SSL encryption. You also can remotely remove an account and the data associated with it, as well as link access to your firm's single sign-on system. Dropbox can log who has accessed each file and make the information available to the system administrator.

WEBSITE: https://www.dropbox.com
FEATURES: https://www.dropbox.com/features

Dropbox

COST

Free Trial Offer:	Yes
Subscription:	Yes
Price:	$9.99 per month starting

AVAILABLE ON

Platform:	Browser-based
	Android
	iOS

SECURITY

2 Factor Authentication:	Yes
Data Security:	Yes
Data Center:	SOC 2 Type II

Other Features

Integration:	Yes
Training:	Yes

Microsoft OneDrive

OVERVIEW:

OneDrive is a secure cloud storage that allows users to store and share photos and videos anywhere via any device, including desktops, laptops, tablets, and mobile phones. This application will enable users to keep their favorite photos and videos safe, even if something happens to their device.

OneDrive works with Microsoft Office and allows users to create, edit, and share their documents quickly. OneDrive supports other collaboration tools such as SharePoint and real-time co-authoring, which would enable users to work with anyone inside or outside of their organization. Users can use built-in search and discovery tools to find relevant files quickly. Storage plans start at $5.00 per user per month for 1 TB of storage and $10 per user per month for unlimited storage.

Files are encrypted when they are stored on Microsoft's servers and encrypted when transmitted. File auditing is also available under its business plan.

WEBSITE: https://onedrive.live.com/
FEATURES:https://www.microsoft.com/en-us/microsoft-365/onedrive/compare-onedrive-plans?activetab=tab:primaryr1

Microsoft OneDrive

COST

Free Trial Offer:	Yes
Subscription:	Yes
Price:	$5.00 per month starting

AVAILABLE ON

Platform:	Browser-based
	Android
	iOS

SECURITY

2 Factor Authentication:	Yes
Data Security:	Yes
Data Center:	SOC 2 Type II

Other Features

Integration:	Yes - with Office365
Training:	Yes

GoogleOne

OVERVIEW:

The Google One platform provides cloud storage space for your files, including work documents, emails, photos, and all file types. Storage is available across Google Drive, Gmail, and Photos, so access to files is easy. Images stored in GoogleOne keep their original resolution, so there is no loss in picture quality.

By storing files in Google One, they can be accessed, shared, edited, any time, and anywhere. Google One also allows you to share your files with people outside your organization to share information and collaborate. Access to the files is across a virtual private network (VPN), ensuring data security in transit.

There is a free plan which provides 15 GB of storage. The highest-paid plan costs $9.99 per user per month and provides 2 TB of storage.

WEBSITE: https://one.google.com/about
FEATURES: https://one.google.com/about/plans

GoogleOne

COST

Free Trial Offer:	Yes
Subscription:	Yes
Price:	15 GB Free 100 GB for $1.99 per month starting

AVAILABLE ON

Platform:	Browser-based
	Android
	iOS

SECURITY

2 Factor Authentication:	Yes
Data Security:	Yes
Data Center:	SOC 2 Type II

Other Features

Integration:	Yes
Training:	Yes

FINANCE

Freshbooks

OVERVIEW:

Freshbooks is a full-featured accounting package built for business owners and their clients. The pricing model of Freshbooks is set by the number of clients you have. The starting package limits invoices to 5 customers and allows for unlimited expense tracking. You can manage payments through the system and set up a credit card or ACH payments. Reporting enables you to handle taxes and see the financial health of the firm. The system includes a mobile device that runs on Android or iOS smartphones. Dashboards give you a single view into the health of your business so you can manage performance.

Other versions of the tool support up to 50, 500, or unlimited clients. As your firm grows and you advance in levels, so will the number of features available in the product. You will have the ability to run business health reports, provide your accountant access to your account, track mileage, send late notices, and set up a recurring payment. All versions include a client self-service portal that enables them to see their account and track payments.

WEBSITE: https://www.freshbooks.com/
FEATURES: https://www.freshbooks.com/pricing

Freshbooks

COST

Free Trial Offer:	Yes
Subscription:	Yes
Price:	Up to 5 clients cost $4.50 per month Up to 50 clients cost $7.50 per month Up to 500 clients cost $150.00 per month Call the company if clients exceed 500

AVAILABLE ON

Platform:	Browser-based
	Android
	iOS

SECURITY

2 Factor Authentication:	Yes
Data Security:	Encrypted in transit
Data Center:	

Other Features

Integration:	Yes - with banks
Training:	Yes

Quickbooks

OVERVIEW:

QuickBooks Online solution puts all your business accounting in one place and makes the information accessible from any workstation or mobile device. The program allows you to track transactions, record mileage, and invoice clients. Quickbooks Online allows you to store your firm's receipts' electronic images, reducing the need for paper files. When properly configured, your customers can pay you through QuickBooks using ACH or PayPal, with the funds going directly to your firm's bank account.

The QuickBooks application can create financial statements, record sales history, record the invoices' status, and generate a balance sheet. The tool also can produce a financial report for your accountant. A central dashboard tool presents the financial health of your company in a single view.

Using QuickBooks, you can share your data with your accountant electronically. This will allow them to generate the data needed to process tax forms in less time. Data in storage and transmission from the server is encrypted to maximize protection.

WEBSITE: https://quickbooks.intuit.com/
FEATURES: https://quickbooks.intuit.com/pricing/

Quickbooks

COST

Free Trial Offer:	Yes
Subscription:	Yes
Price:	$7.50 per month

AVAILABLE ON

Platform:	Browser-based
	Android
	iOS

SECURITY

2 Factor Authentication:	Yes
Data Security:	Yes
Data Center:	SOC 2 Type II

Other Features

Integration:	Yes - with banks
Training:	Yes

Xero

OVERVIEW:

Xero offers features that let you run every aspect of your business from a single application. Using the tool, you can track the time and expenses associated with a case. Manage your client invoicing and receive electronic payment for services. The software also has a feature that allows it to interface with your bank to reconcile your account. You can run reports and view the status of your business using its dashboards.

The application also has a mobile application that allows you to capture expenses and time using your mobile device. You can maintain a contact list, manage your business assets, and store files within the system. Xero can convert foreign currency transactions into your local currency.

The features of Xero are available to unlimited users. The cost is set based on the number of invoices and the features you need. The "Early" level is for a new business just starting and contains all the essential features you need to manage your business. The "Growing" level has unlimited invoices, and the "Established" level includes the ability to track time and costs by project, track expenses, and multi-currency transactions.

WEBSITE: https://www.xero.com/us/
FEATURES: https://www.xero.com/us/pricing/

Xero

COST

Free Trial Offer:	Yes
Subscription:	Yes
Price:	Early level is $9 per month Growing level is $30 per month Established level is $60 per month

AVAILABLE ON

Platform:	Browser-based
	Android
	iOS

SECURITY

2 Factor Authentication:	Yes
Data Security:	Encrypted at rest and in transit
Data Center:	SOC 2

Other Features

Integration:	Yes - with banks
Training:	Yes

INTEGRATION

Automate.io

OVERVIEW:
Are you tired of duplicative data entry? Would you like the data from one program to be copied to another program automatically? Automate.io allows you to integrate data between two applications without writing any code. You can design these interfaces to run automatically several times a day or hour based on your need.

When would you use automate.io? Let's say you have a Google Form that collects information from potential clients. You can use Automate.io to copy that person's email into Mailchimp to add them to your mail list, and they can receive copies of your newsletters or emails. Or, you can use Automate.io to copy your email into Trello or Square. You can leverage the library of automation scripts already designed between over 200 applications using the Automate.io library. The automation can also contain conditional logic or time delays, which allow you to achieve various integrations.

Automate.io is priced based on the number of integrations you program and the frequency in which they run. A free version of the product, with a limited number of automations, is available for free. Automate.io will save you time and money from administrative tasks, allowing you to focus on your customers.
WEBSITE: https://automate.io/zapieralternative
FEATURES: https://automate.io/pricing

Automate.io

COST

Free Trial Offer:	Yes
Subscription:	Yes
Price:	Free version: 300 actions, 5 Bots, Data Check 5 minutes Personal version: 2,000 actions, 20 Bots, Data Check 5 minutes Cost $29 per month Startup Version: 10,000 actions, 50 Bots, Data Check 2 minutes Cost $49 per month Growth Version 30,000 actions, 100 Bots, Data Check 2 minutes Cost $99 per month Business Version:100,000 actions, 200 Bots, Data Check 1 minutes Cost $199 per month Executive Version: 500,000 actions, unlimited Bots, Data Check 1 minutes Cost $399 per month

AVAILABLE ON

Platform:	Browser-based

SECURITY

2 Factor Authentication:	
Data Security:	Data Encryption at rest and transit
Data Center:	

Other Features

Integration:	Yes
Training:	Yes

Integromat

OVERVIEW:
Integromat unique architecture gives you the power to integrate applications into complex workflows, which will automate your business's administrative tasks. You can choose from predefined templates or custom develop your integration using the Integromat editor. Integromat can route or aggregate processes based on the information contained in the triggered event. You also have the unique ability to conduct error handling for events, which allows you to deal with unexpected exceptions to your process. The service can handle errors in several ways, based on the commands you give the workflow.

Using the Integromat editor, you can develop your workflows without any programming knowledge. In addition to integrating applications, Integromat will also interface with hardware devices like smartphones. You can define actions to occur based on the smartphone's GPS location, when text messages are sent or received, and even when the user connects to a wifi signal. Many of these features are available for Android and iOS devices. Another unique feature of Integromat is the ability to interact with applications via web services. Using the JSON or HTTP/SOAP protocol, you can interact with almost any application that has a web service. Advanced features require programming skills.

WEBSITE: https://www.integromat.com/en
FEATURES: https://www.integromat.com/en/features

Integromat

COST

Free Trial Offer:	Yes
Subscription:	Yes
Price:	Free version with limited functionality Pricing based on operations and frequency

AVAILABLE ON

Platform:	Browser-based

SECURITY

2 Factor Authentication:	Yes
Data Security:	Encryption for data at rest and transit
Data Center:	

Other Features

Integration:	Yes
Training:	Yes

Zapier

OVERVIEW:

If you have ever needed to share data between two tools but did not want to re-enter data, then Zapier is the tool for you. Using the Zapier tool, you can create triggers called a "Zap" to take predefined action on a preset schedule. An example of a "trigger" could be sending you a text message every time you receive an email from a particular person. Zapier can create Zaps between over 300 applications using their easy to use web-based interface. Once you create a “Zap,” you can determine if you want it to run multiple times an hour, daily, weekly, or monthly.

The web-based tool allows you to create Zaps, turn them on and off, manage access to different applications, and set the Zap schedule. Creating a Zap does not require any coding knowledge as Zapier’s application handles the application APIs needed to develop the Zaps and automate them.

Another advantage of Zapier is the knowledge of the user community that uses the product. They provide the company with feedback on the application, which leads to future product development.

WEBSITE: https://zapier.com/
FEATURES: https://zapier.com/pricing

Zapier

COST

Free Trial Offer:	Yes
Subscription:	Yes
Price:	Free starting 100 Tasks per month

AVAILABLE ON

Platform:	Browser-based

SECURITY

2 Factor Authentication:	Yes
Data Security:	Yes
Data Center:	Working to achieve SOC 2 Type II

Other Features

Integration:	Yes
Training:	Yes

MARKETING

Constant Contact

OVERVIEW:

Constant Contact is an email marketing tool that enables you to produce professional marketing campaigns with minimal technical skills. Through the use of online tools, you can create professional emails without the need to code. You can brand your emails with your firm's logo or use graphics from their library of public use images.

Constant Contact will help you grow your business, build customer relationships, and find new leads. You can create forms designed to capture additional information and qualify your prospective lead. This information will help you build multi-message campaigns to market your services.

The suite of tools includes Email Marketing, Social Campaigns, Save Local, Event Marketing, and Online Survey. Constant contact also can manage your marketing lists, allowing customers to subscribe and unsubscribe from the list without you having to do any data entry. Other features include sending coupons, conducting polls and surveys, and having dynamic content.

WEBSITE: https://www.constantcontact.com

FEATURES: https://www.constantcontact.com/pricing-info

Constant Contact

COST

Free Trial Offer:	Yes
Subscription:	Yes
Price:	$20 per month

AVAILABLE ON

Platform:	Browser-based

SECURITY

2 Factor Authentication:	Yes
Data Security:	Yes
Data Center:	

Other Features

Integration:	Yes
Training:	Yes

Google Ads

OVERVIEW:

This marketing tool offered by Google is unique as it posts your advertisements for free. You only pay when someone clicks on your ad. You will only pay for qualified leads, which gives you a higher percentage of turning your clicks into customers. Ads are displayed when people conduct searches on Google, and costs do not exceed your advertising budget.

The price you pay for a click is determined by the area you are marketing to and the number of competing customers in that market who will see the ad. For example, if you are marketing family law to customers in a major city, you will pay more than running the same ad in a rural area. Also, narrowing your market to Google searches for family law will help you find qualified leads. Your advertisements continue to display until the budget you set with Google runs out of money.

You have complete control over when the ads are displayed. The active display time can be set to a particular time of day, zip code, or season. No long-term contracts are signed; you simply control when the ads are turned on or off and based on your account's funding.

WEBSITE: https://ads.google.com
FEATURES:

Google Ads

COST

Free Trial Offer:	No
Subscription:	Budget based
Price:	Pay as you go, charged when someone clicks on your advertisement

AVAILABLE ON

Platform:	Browser-based
	Android
	iOS

SECURITY

2 Factor Authentication:	Yes
Data Security:	
Data Center:	

Other Features

Integration:	Yes
Training:	

LinkedIn

OVERVIEW:
Most people do not think of LinkedIn for marketing, but it has truly become the modern-day business card and business networking tool. When you meet with a new client, do you ever check their LinkedIn account to learn more about them? Do you see if you have a common interest to discuss as an ice breaker in your meeting? Don't underestimate the power of LinkedIn in representing your accomplishments, creating business relationships, and increasing your knowledge.

Many people don't realize LinkedIn has many features available to people who pay for their premium service offerings. For example, you can use search engines to find people within a company, find people who share familiar friends, or even alumni of your school or past employers. LinkedIn also contains training material, company insight, salary information, and job announcements. As an attorney, you can conduct research for your clients without ever leaving your desk to help you prepare a case.
Use LinkedIn to show prospective clients the unique services you provide. Include references from clients you have helped in the past and highlight professional associations. Use LinkedIn to comment on news articles, share blogs on recent cases, and show how you are a leader in your industry.
WEBSITE: https://premium.linkedin.com/
FEATURES: https://business.linkedin.com/

LinkedIn

COST

Free Trial Offer:	Yes
Subscription:	Free Subscription plus Premium
Price:	Free Subscription Job Seekers - $29.99 to $59.99 per month Sales Professionals - $64.99 per month Recruiter - $99.95 per month

AVAILABLE ON

Platform:	Browser-based
	Android
	iOS

SECURITY

2 Factor Authentication:	Yes
Data Security:	Data encrypted in transit
Data Center:	SOC 2

Other Features

Integration:	Yes
Training:	Yes

MailChimp

OVERVIEW:
Designed as an automation platform, MailChimp allows you to create, send, and analyze email associated with marketing campaigns. MailChimp lets you create custom templates and, at the same time, choose from an array of pre-made templates and campaigns. Customers can brand their messages with their logo or add custom images. You can measure the marketing campaign's overall effectiveness by seeing how many times the user opens the message or clicks on its links.

MailChimp also can develop a multi-message campaign that sends many emails over a predetermined period. An example of this is email campaigns in which each message builds on the preceding message. Each message is an opportunity to educate the customer and get your firm's name in front of them by building trust and brand recognition.

Using the MailChimp platform, you can manage up to 2,000 contacts without any financial commitment. The MailChimp mobile application gives you the power to create and send campaigns, manage subscribers, keep tabs on your account activity, and more from your phone. Additional features offered by the company include design tools and website hosting.

WEBSITE: https://mailchimp.com/
FEATURES: https://mailchimp.com/pricing/

MailChimp

COST

Free Trial Offer:	Yes
Subscription:	Yes
Price:	Free Version Paid Version starts at $10 per month

AVAILABLE ON

Platform:	Browser-based
	Android
	iOS

SECURITY

2 Factor Authentication:	Yes
Data Security:	PCI for credit card transactions
Data Center:	SOC II

Other Features

Integration:	Yes
Training:	

Unbundled Attorney

OVERVIEW:

Unbundled Attorney handles the marketing part of your business, allowing you to focus on your cases. The service provides a web-based tool that will market your legal services to people seeking legal advice. Based on the type of assistance the prospective client is seeking and their geographic location, Unbundled Attorney will refer the lead to you if it is a good match. The service acts as your business development department, helping to find clients that need the type of legal service you provide in the marketplace.

Their system focuses on using search engine optimization to find leads. Unbundled Attorney also pre-qualifies the leads before sending you the referral, increasing the percentage of new clients you receive.

WEBSITE: https://www.unbundledattorney.com/
FEATURES:

Unbundled Attorney

COST

Free Trial Offer:	
Subscription:	
Price:	Need to contact

AVAILABLE ON

Platform:	Browser-based
	Android
	iOS

SECURITY

2 Factor Authentication:	
Data Security:	
Data Center:	

Other Features

Integration:	
Training:	

NOTE TOOLS

Evernote

OVERVIEW:

Do you ever wish you could eliminate the need to capture information on notepaper or wish you had to access your notes anytime and on any device? Evernote is a tool that allows you to capture information in note form, save it to a system that is fully searchable on a computer or mobile device. Notes can be any type of information such as emails, pictures, handwritten notes, web clips, or even scanned documents. Evernote indexes the info so any piece of information, no matter how small, is fully searchable. It even can search handwritten notes and PDFs that you save to the tool.

Evernote tools allow you to capture the information you see displayed in your computer's web browser, use templates to standardize how you capture information, and scan documents. Evernote is used to share information within your teams by granting permissions to other users creating a shared knowledge database for families, co-workers, and project teams.

Pricing is free for one user and two devices. You are limited to a note size of 25 MB and a 60 MB monthly upload limit. The premium package starts at $7.99 per month and allows access to unlimited devices and a note size of 200 MB with a 10 GB monthly upload limit.

WEBSITE: https://evernote.com/
FEATURES: https://evernote.com/compare-plans

Evernote

COST

Free Trial Offer:	Yes
Subscription:	Yes
Price:	Basic is free Premium is $7.99 per month Business is $14.99 per user per month

AVAILABLE ON

Platform:	Browser-based
	Android
	iOS

SECURITY

2 Factor Authentication:	Yes
Data Security:	Data is encrypted
Data Center:	SAS 70 (Type II) and SSAE SOC-1 (Type 2) Certified

Other Features

Integration:	Yes
Training:	Yes

OneNote

OVERVIEW:

OneNote is Microsoft's note application, which allows you to capture information from many sources into one location. Using a notebook analogy, OneNote allows you to create notebooks (individual files) that contain sections and pages to organize information. You can edit your notes using colors and fonts, include images, add hyperlinks to content on the web, or even draw with a stylus or mouse. OneNote notebooks can be shared with other users, making them the perfect tools for teams.

OneNote's additional features include recording meetings, generating to-do lists, and adding tags to information. Built-in search capability can locate information within a single notebook or across multiple books. Information stored in OneNote is retrievable from a desktop computer or mobile device.

Information can be entered into OneNote by using a web extension tool that makes copying information easy. OneNote automatically captures the rich text from the web site and stores it with the original website's URL. You can also store file types of different content like audio files, videos, and working documents. OneNote files can be stored on your local computer or in your Microsoft OneDrive, allowing you to share information with people you grant permission.

WEBSITE: http://www.onenote.com

OneNote

COST

Free Trial Offer:	Yes
Subscription:	No
Price:	OneNote is Free

AVAILABLE ON

Platform:	Browser-based
	Android
	iOS

SECURITY

2 Factor Authentication:	Yes
Data Security:	SOC 2 Type II
Data Center:	Yes

Other Features

Integration:	Yes
Training:	Yes

PDF MANAGEMENT

Adobe Document Cloud

OVERVIEW:
Adobe Document Cloud (DC) is the packaging Adobe subscription software that bundles their most popular products. With the Document Cloud, you get the Adobe desktop software, mobile scan application, signature application, and the Acobrate mobile reader application. Because you are operating in the cloud, you also can store and share files online, enable workflows for sending, e-signing, and track the status of documents.

Using the Adobe tools, you can convert any kind of document into a PDF. You can also merge multiple PDFs into a single PDF document, which can simplify your document management. The program allows you to create fillable PDF forms shared securely with co-workers or people outside your organization. You can also comment on PDFs using text editing, highlighters, and sticky note tools. Passwords and permissions are applied to PDFs to restrict editing and copying rights and protect them from unauthorized access. All of these features are accessible from smartphones and tablets in addition to a desktop computer.

WEBSITE:
https://acrobat.adobe.com/us/en/?promoid=CRH529QL&mv=other

FEATURES:https://acrobat.adobe.com/us/en/acrobat/pricing.html?promoid=DZTH12D8&mv=other

Adobe Document Cloud

COST

Free Trial Offer:	Yes
Subscription:	Yes
Price:	$14.99 per month

AVAILABLE ON

Platform:	Browser-based
	Android
	iOS

SECURITY

2 Factor Authentication:	Yes
Data Security:	Encryption is available
Data Center:	SOC2

Other Features

Integration:	Yes
Training:	Yes

PROJECT MANAGEMENT

LeanKit

OVERVIEW:

LeanKit is a tool that allows you to manage tasks using the KanBan project management method. Using this method, you categorize each task on a card into one of three columns: “To-Do,” “Doing Now,” and “Finished.” You prioritize cards by moving them to the top of the column and then through the three columns as you work on them. The key to KanBan is to limit the number of “Doing Now” tasks you are working on to stay focused. When a “Doing Now” task is “Finished” you pull a new card from your “To-Do” column. Kanban allows you to focus your energy on a limited number of tasks, which increases your productivity.

LeanKit automates the KanBan process to help your firm manage its workload. You can attach due dates and files to each card, allowing you to keep all the information you need in one place. You may also customize columns to duplicate court or business processes to track the motions you are working on. You can share your LeanKit board with team members in your firm so you can focus on completing the same issues.

The LeanKit application is available via a browser or through a mobile application on your phone.

WEBSITE: https://leankit.com/
FEATURES: https://www.planview.com/products-solutions/products/leankit/

LeanKit

COST

Free Trial Offer:	Yes
Subscription:	Yes
Price:	$20 per user per month

AVAILABLE ON

Platform:	Browser-based
	Android
	iOS

SECURITY

2 Factor Authentication:	
Data Security:	Data is encrypted
Data Center:	SOC 2 Type II

Other Features

Integration:	Yes
Training:	Yes

Trello

OVERVIEW:

Trello is a project management tool based on the KanBan project management methodology. In Trello, you categorize each task on a card into one of three columns: "To-Do," "Doing," and "Done." You prioritize cards by moving them to the top of the column and then through the three columns as you work on them. Trello improves your project management by helping you to limit the number of "Doing" tasks so you stay focused.

Trello allows you to add comments, attachments, and due dates to each task card. You can also use built-in workflow tools to automate your work, so your cards' changes reflect milestones or due dates. You can create custom boards that mimic your internal workflow process, so you know every action's status. Trello integrates with other applications, allowing you to link to cloud storage solutions, note applications, and more.

Through the use of Trello's mobile application, you can be in sync with your tasks no matter where you are. Team members can also use Trello to keep everyone focused on the tasks and improve productivity.

WEBSITE: https://trello.com/
FEATURES: https://trello.com/pricing

Trello

COST

Free Trial Offer:	Yes
Subscription:	Yes
Price:	Free per user per month $9.88 per user per month Business Class $17.50 per user per month for Enterprise

AVAILABLE ON

Platform:	Browser-based
	Android / iOS

SECURITY

2 Factor Authentication:	Yes
Data Security:	Data encryption at rest and in transit
Data Center:	SOC 2

Other Features

Integration:	Yes
Training:	Yes

PASSWORD MANAGERS

1Password

OVERVIEW:

Are you tired of creating unique passwords for every application you use? Do you wish you could have only one password for all your applications without creating a significant security risk? 1Password is a solution that allows you to create one master password to your password vault. When your vault is open, and you access a protected website, 1 Password with insert your username and unique password to help you gain access. Now each site can have a unique complex password, and you only have to remember one password.

You can store usernames and passwords for every website, shipping information, credit cards, confidential documents, contracts, and private notes within your vault. The same master password will grant you access to everything you place within your vault. If you purchase the family or business version, you will also have the ability to share passwords. Family members will have access to the passwords you share.

Using 1Password, you can also generate complex passwords for sites. The application will integrate with your browser as an extension, making access to your vault easy. Deleted items can also be restored within a year of deletion.

WEBSITE: https://1password.com/
FEATURES: https://1password.com/sign-up/

1 Password

COST

Free Trial Offer:	Yes
Subscription:	Yes
Price:	$2.99 per user per month starting $7.99 per user per month for Business

AVAILABLE ON

Platform:	Browser-based
	Android
	iOS

SECURITY

2 Factor Authentication:	Yes
Data Security:	Data encrypted at rest and transit
Data Center:	

Other Features

Integration:	Yes
Training:	

Google Password Manager

OVERVIEW:

The Chrome browser allows you to store usernames and passwords within your Chrome browser or Android device. Chrome detects when you are entering a Username/Password and offers to save it to their server. If you are a Chrome user, the advantage is you never have to leave your website to access your account. Your existing Google account provides you with one password access to the password manager.

Google Password Manager will not work in other browsers, so you lose the ability to access your passwords in Internet Explorer or Edge. Also, the password manager will not work natively on IOS mobile devices. But, if you use multiple Google devices like an Android phone, desktop browser, or Chromebook, your passwords will automatically sync across devices.

The Google password manager can generate strong passwords for your websites, and you can export the information to a spreadsheet if needed. You can also set the Auto Sign-in feature to automatically sign you into a website by-passing the username/password prompt.

WEBSITE:
https://support.google.com/accounts/answer/6197437?hl=en
FEATURES:

Google Password Manager

COST

Free Trial Offer:	Yes
Subscription:	Yes
Price:	Free

AVAILABLE ON

Platform:	Browser-based
	Android

SECURITY

2 Factor Authentication:	Yes
Data Security:	Encrypted in storage and transit
Data Center:	

Other Features

Integration:	Yes
Training:	No

Dashlane

OVERVIEW:

Dashlane is an enterprise password security solution designed to help individuals and companies manage usernames/passwords and prevent bad password habits. The tool utilizes a patented security architecture that encrypts usernames and passwords, so data remains protected. Passwords are accessible from Android and iOS devices, as well as through a web browser.

The Dashlane tool saves your passwords and logins as you access different applications. If you need to generate a secure password, the password generator tool will create a unique password for your use. The next time you access the website, Dashlane will automatically enter your username and password, saving you time.

Dashlane also allows you to manage multiple accounts under its business plans. The business plan has a dashboard that will enable you to identify password issues (too few characters or password repeats), so you can encourage your team to improve their security over time. Dashlane will also integrate with a company's single sign-on security application.

WEBSITE: https://www.dashlane.com/
FEATURES: https://www.dashlane.com/plans

Dashlane

COST

Free Trial Offer:	Yes
Subscription:	Yes
Price:	Free for up to 50 passwords. $4.99 per user per month individual plan $14.00 per month family plan

AVAILABLE ON

Platform:	Browser-based
	Android
	iOS

SECURITY

2 Factor Authentication:	Yes
Data Security:	Data encrypted at rest and in transit.
Data Center:	

Other Features

Integration:	Yes
Training:	

Lastpass

OVERVIEW:
LastPass is a cloud-based service that provides a central location to manage usernames and passwords for applications. The tool also allows you to store information about credit cards and notes, all encrypted with a single password that only you know. Entering the master password for LastPass unlocks all the tool's capabilities, giving you the ability to see your information on your computer or your mobile device.

LastPass also provides the ability to share your information with selected users in your account through the concept of shared folders. Your team or family will have access to the same protected information, eliminating duplicate entries.

Through a dashboard, LastPass can provide a status of passwords' health, identifying which ones are reused or not considered substantial. LastPass can also generate strong passwords for you, helping you to implement password best practices.

Download LastPass as a browser extension or a mobile application onto your iOS or Android device. Because your information is stored encrypted in the cloud, all your devices stay synced.

WEBSITE: https://www.lastpass.com
FEATURES: https://www.lastpass.com/pricing

LastPass

COST

Free Trial Offer:	Yes
Subscription:	Yes
Price:	Free for Single User $3 per user per month for Premium $4 per month for families and Premium Business plans available

AVAILABLE ON

Platform:	Browser-based
	Android
	iOS

SECURITY

2 Factor Authentication:	Yes
Data Security:	Encrypted at rest and transit
Data Center:	

Other Features

Integration:	Yes
Training:	

STAFFING / HR

BambooHR

OVERVIEW:

Do you need an HR system to help you manage your workforce? BambooHR has many features designed to save you time and make you more productive. You can use the tool to hire new employees by using it to create offer letters, generate employee packets, and collect signatures. You can even use the software and its email features to negotiate compensation and interact quickly with applicants.

After onboarding a new person, BambooHR will allow you to track their benefits, leave, and performance. Managers can set performance goals, and employees can rate their performance and that of their peers. You can also use the tool to gather input from employees on training plans and measure job satisfaction.

BambooHR will allow employees to request time off and see the master office schedule. Managers can approve leave and track employee training. The system is also capable of tracking employee time by project through a timesheet function. The system is also available via a mobile device, which provides greater interaction for employee transparency.

WEBSITE: https://www.bamboohr.com/
FEATURES: https://www.bamboohr.com/packaging/

BambooHR

COST

Free Trial Offer:	Yes
Subscription:	Yes
Price:	Not published

AVAILABLE ON

Platform:	Browser-based
	Android
	iOS

SECURITY

2 Factor Authentication:	
Data Security:	Yes
Data Center:	SOC 2 Type II

Other Features

Integration:	Yes
Training:	Yes

Lawclerk

OVERVIEW:

Need temporary help for a big case, or an attorney with a unique skill set? LAWCLERK allows you to find and work with on-demand associates who are paid by the project. The process of using LAWCLERK is simple, you post a team application, lawyers apply, and then you select the best members to form your team. Using the tool, you can post a confidential project, set a flat fee, and wait for attorneys interested in your project to apply. The advantage of using LAWCLERK is you can grow your practice as your requirements change without entering into a long term employment relationship.

If you are an attorney looking for work, you can also post your resume on the site and connect with firms looking to fill their labor needs. Because the work is virtual, you can work on your schedule from any location. Probably the most significant advantage of LAWCLERK for an attorney looking for a job is you get to decide which type of cases you want to work on. LAWCLERK acts as the middleman to guarantee payment for the work you performed.

WEBSITE: https://www.lawclerk.legal/

Lawclerk

COST

Free Trial Offer:	Yes
Subscription:	Yes
Price:	Cost based on engagement

AVAILABLE ON

Platform:	Browser-based

SECURITY

2 Factor Authentication:	
Data Security:	Encryption
Data Center:	

Other Features

Integration:	
Training:	Yes

TIME TRACKING

Chrometa

OVERVIEW:

Chrometa runs in your computer's background and records how you spend your time - acting as your timekeeper with no manual record-keeping or notes. It will record which applications you were working in and what tasks you performed. For example, it can tell you which people you sent an email to during the day and how long you spend composing the messages. It then provides the information to you through their time report generator based on the parameters you set.

Chrometa also can link keywords to project codes, so you can track how long you were working on a legal matter for your client. The result of using the tool is an accurate timesheet with all activity linked to a project code. Chrometa saves you the daily tasks of tracking your time and thus frees you to work on other activities.

Data from Chrometa can be exported to other 3rd party applications to facilitate the billing process. It also integrates with other case management tools to eliminate duplicative data entry, such as adding clients. Data is transmitted across a secure virtual private network (VPN) to protect the data in transit.

WEBSITE: https://www.chrometa.com/
FEATURES:https://chrometa.com/time-tracking-for-law-firms.html

Chrometa

COST

Free Trial Offer:	Yes
Subscription:	Yes
Price:	$19 per user per month starting

AVAILABLE ON

Platform:	Browser-based
	Android
	iOS

SECURITY

2 Factor Authentication:	Yes
Data Security:	Yes
Data Center:	SOC 2 Type II

Other Features

Integration:	Yes
Training:	Yes

ClockShark

OVERVIEW:

ClockShark has features that make tracking your time easy. Attorneys can enter their time into the application and be approved by a supervisor if necessary. The tool provides reporting capabilities that provide insight into time allocation by project code. You also can attach photos or notes to the timesheet to account for time. The project can set limits so you can be alert when non-billable work is about to be performed. The ability to set budget alerts exist if you are hiring and tracking additional support personnel for work on large cases.

Data can be entered on a mobile device, and make the timesheet available 24/7/365. An exciting feature of the tool is GPS-fencing, which can send reminders to attorneys to enter their time as they enter or leave a facility. Alerts can notify supervisors when hours are missing from the system.

The integration capability of ClockShark allows you to export data to several financial tools for payroll and accounting. These 3rd party systems can use time report data to generate invoices and manage payments, reducing your time tracking tasks.

WEBSITE: https://www.clockshark.com/
FEATURES:https://www.clockshark.com/Pricing/

ClockShark

COST

Free Trial Offer:	Yes
Subscription:	Yes
Price:	The basic package costs $3 per user per month The standard package costs $6 per user per month The Pro Package costs $8 per user per month.

AVAILABLE ON

Platform:	Browser-based
	Android
	iOS

SECURITY

2 Factor Authentication:	
Data Security:	unknown
Data Center:	

Other Features

Integration:	Yes
Training:	Yes

TimeTracker

OVERVIEW:

TimeTracker's goal is to reduce the administrative costs associated with tracking time and help your firm be more profitable. TimeTracker accomplished this goal by offering a product with features that allow you to capture time and costs by client. Using their tool, you can have employees complete timesheets, track days off in a group calendar, use ABA codes to track expenses, and generate alerts if someone forgets to enter their time. Through a web-based or mobile application, you can access these functions on smartphone devices.

To help you manage your business, you can run reports against the data and track your client's time. TimeTracker offers the ability to integrate with external account and payroll applications to eliminate duplicative data entry. More advanced versions of the offering include features that allow you to generate invoices directly from the application and securely manage online payments.

TimeTracker has advanced features that will allow you to manage trust accounts and provide your customers with a client portal. A customized dashboard will enable you to see all the information you need to run your business in one location.

WEBSITE: https://www.ebillity.com/
FEATURES: https://www.ebillity.com/time-tracker-legal/

TimeTracker

COST

Free Trial Offer:	Yes
Subscription:	Yes
Price:	Time Tracker level costs $4 per user per month Billing level costs $8 per user per month Legal Version level costs $12 per user/month

AVAILABLE ON

Platform:	Browser-based
	Android
	iOS

SECURITY

2 Factor Authentication:	
Data Security:	Encrypted in transit
Data Center:	

Other Features

Integration:	Yes
Training:	Yes

TELEPHONY

NEXA

OVERVIEW:

NEXA is a virtual receptionist that provides many features designed to satisfy your client's needs. You can establish customer-specific scripting for calls, have coverage 24 x 7 x 365, get real-time reporting and analytics, and have the virtual receptionist provide simple scheduling for your staff. NEXA sets its cost at a monthly rate plus a per-minute charge, so you only pay for the service you use, helping to reduce your cost.

NEXA also establishes a local and toll-free number for their service, allowing your customers to reach you from anywhere. Depending on the time of day, the virtual receptionist can forward calls or take a message. The Enterprise plan also integrates customer relationship management programs, lead intake, and even follow-up services.

The receptionist is trained to know your industry and can provide context information to interact with your customers. Nexa's mobile application and portal allows you to track your calls and manage your business.

WEBSITE: https://nexa.com/
FEATURES: https://nexa.com/plans/

NEXA

COST

Free Trial Offer:	Yes
Subscription:	Yes
Price:	Starting at $99 per month plus $1.50 per minute

AVAILABLE ON

Platform:	Browser-based
	Android
	iOS

SECURITY

2 Factor Authentication:	
Data Security:	
Data Center:	

Other Features

Integration:	Yes
Training:	Yes

Ruby Receptionist

OVERVIEW:

Ruby Receptionist is a virtual receptionist in which your calls are answered by a professional receptionist who interacts with your customers, leaving a positive user experience. Using a desktop application, you can decide when to forward your calls to Ruby Receptionist or answer them yourself. You can also integrate the service with your customer relationship management software so the receptionist can provide personalized service.

The service allows you to have a custom greeting, route calls by type, complete customer intake forms, and provide bilingual answering services. Ruby Receptionist will even schedule appointments, provide local and toll-free numbers and voicemail transcriptions.

Ruby Receptionist's mobile application allows you to set your availability and preferences and track customer activity. You can even call and text your customers from your business phone number directly from the application.

WEBSITE: https://www.callruby.com/
FEATURES: https://www.ruby.com/plans-and-pricing/

Ruby Receptionist

COST

Free Trial Offer:	No
Subscription:	Yes
Price:	Packages start at $199 for 50 minutes per month

AVAILABLE ON

Platform:	Browser-based
	Android
	iOS

SECURITY

2 Factor Authentication:	
Data Security:	
Data Center:	

Other Features

Integration:	Yes
Training:	

TRANSCRIPTION

Rev

OVERVIEW:

Used by many industries, Rev specialized in converting audio and video files to text through their online transcription service. In addition to transcription, they can provide captioning for videos and translation services.

After you create an account, you will have the ability to upload your audio or video files to the Rev portal. They will then distribute the work to their team of transcribers, convert the information to text, and present you with an editable document. Rec guarantees an accuracy standard of 99% for this work, reviewed before delivery to their customer. The rate for translation is $1.25 per audio minute.

Their network of transcribes is so extensive that they can deliver transcriptions within 12 hours for most files that are less than 30 minutes in length. They can also provide a rush delivery of 4 hours for most files less than 30 minutes at additional cost.

WEBSITE: https://www.rev.com/
FEATURES: https://www.rev.com/transcription

Rev

COST

Free Trial Offer:	No
Subscription:	No
Price:	Standard: $1.25 per audio minute

AVAILABLE ON

Platform:	Browser-based
	Android
	iOS

SECURITY

2 Factor Authentication:	
Data Security:	Encryption of files at rest and in transit
Data Center:	

Other Features

Integration:	
Training:	Yes

Speakwrite

OVERVIEW:

Do you ever need transcription services for your legal cases? SpeakWrite will convert your recorded audio into written text in about 3 hours simply by sending them an audio file across the internet. The service is available 24 /7, and there are no minimum page lengths. You pay as little as 1.5 cents per word.

Using the SpeakWrite portal, you can submit an audio file to their translators. The service can use templates, or a personal worklist (acronyms), to make the translations meaningful. SpeakWrite even offers translation services for an additional cost.

Using the Speakwrite mobile application, you can capture audio file recordings from your phone and send them securely to the service for translation. SpeakWrite secures your files with encryption on their server, or when the file travels across the internet.

The company has been providing transcription services since 1997 and specializes in legal and law enforcement transcription services.

WEBSITE: http://speakwrite.com/
FEATURES: https://speakwrite.com/features/

SpeakWrite

COST

Free Trial Offer:	Yes
Subscription:	No
Price:	1.5 cents per word starting for a single speaker 2.25 cents per word for two or more speakers

AVAILABLE ON

Platform:	Browser-based
	Android
	iOS

SECURITY

2 Factor Authentication:	Yes
Data Security:	Encryption of files at rest and in transit
Data Center:	

Other Features

Integration:	
Training:	Yes

TRAVEL

Tripit

OVERVIEW:

TripIt is a travel management tool that allows you to capture all your trip information in one place and make it available on your desktop or mobile device. You can email your airline, hotel, and rental car information to your personal Tripit account, and it will create a virtual itinerary for your trip. When you travel, all your confirmation numbers are in one location and available on your mobile device.

Tripit will also sync with your calendar, help you find nearby hotels and transportation options. It also can supplement your travel information with the weather, maps, and other information to make your trip as easy as possible. Tripit can also let you rate your in-flight experience, tally travel states like days on the road, and show neighborhood safety scores.

You can purchase the premium version called TripIt Pro, and have access to real-time flight alerts, displays security wait times, airport maps, and baggage claim information. You can even use the program to track travel reward programs and update people on changes to your travel plans.

WEBSITE:https://www.tripit.com/web
FEATURES: https://www.tripit.com/web/pro/pricing/

Tripit

COST

Free Trial Offer:	Yes
Subscription:	No
Price:	Basic - Free Pro is $49 per year

AVAILABLE ON

Platform:	Browser-based
	Android
	iOS

SECURITY

2 Factor Authentication:	
Data Security:	Encrypted on a mobile device
Data Center:	

Other Features

Integration:	Yes
Training:	Yes

WRITING TOOLS

Grammarly

OVERVIEW:

Grammarly does more than check your spelling and punctuation; it gives you the tools to be a better writer. Not only will Grammarly help you with grammar, but it also gives you a reader's view of your writing help you to improve your ability to communicate. It can tell you if the paper is clear, engages the readers, and determines the tone and writing style by analyzing your word use. In the paid version, Grammarly will even check for plagiarism.

Integrated into your browser, Grammarly can provide instant feedback on your written work. You can also get a download that integrates the tool into MS Word and MS Outlook. As you write, Grammarly will mark errors with red underlines. You can hover over the error at any point in your writing process and either accept or reject the suggestion.

Grammarly offers a free and premium version of their product. The paid version provides analysis beyond the basic spelling, grammar, and punctuation review of your writing. A business version of the product is also available, providing centralized billing, email support, and integration with your corporate single sign-on solution.

WEBSITE: https://www.grammarly.com/
FEATURES: https://www.grammarly.com/plans

Grammarly

COST

Free Trial Offer:	Yes
Subscription:	Yes
Price:	Free Premium starts at $11.66 per month Business starts at $12.50 per user per month

AVAILABLE ON

Platform:	Browser-based
	Android
	iOS

SECURITY

2 Factor Authentication:	Yes
Data Security:	
Data Center:	SOC 2 - Type I

Other Features

Integration:	Yes
Training:	

PerfectIT

OVERVIEW:
PerfectIt is professional editing software that checks your writing for mistakes that cannot be caught by spelling or grammar checking programs. PerfectIT will check for:

- Abbreviations: Perfect brings clarity by linking every abbreviation to its definition. It automatically generates a Table of Abbreviations.
- Capitalization: PerfectIt checks for inconsistent capitalization in your writing.
- House Style: This includes phrases to avoid, uniform branding, and style preferences, so the document speaks with one voice.
- Hyphens/Dashes: PerfectIt can simplify the tedious task of finding hyphenated words and enforce consistency.
- Bullets and Lists: enforce consistent punctuation and table punctuation.
- Spelling, Typos, and numbers: Perfect approaches spelling differently, looking at a combination of context and common errors.
- Table/Figure Numbering: Automatically detects table and figure numbering for the correct order and headings.

PerfectIt helps customers speak with a consistent voice. It enables multiple writers to follow the corporate standards that make your firm look and sound its best.

WEBSITE: https://intelligentediting.com/
FEATURES:
https://intelligentediting.com/product/introduction/

PerfectIt

COST

Free Trial Offer:	Yes
Subscription:	Yes
Price:	$70 per year starting

AVAILABLE ON

Platform:	Browser-based
	Android
	iOS

SECURITY

2 Factor Authentication:	
Data Security:	
Data Center:	

Other Features

Integration:	
Training:	Yes

Textexpander

OVERVIEW:

Textexpander lets you store snippets of text (signature block, address information, etc) in the cloud, allowing you to access the information at any time to create documents faster and with greater consistency. For example, instead of typing your business address, you can replace it with a Textexpander code. TextExpander will automatically detect the code and replace it with the standardized text you have linked to your code. The tool not only improves consistency by eliminating the chances for errors but more importantly, it saves you time from having to rewrite the same text over and over.

By storing information in the cloud, you can use your codes across multiple devices and platforms. Textexpander codes can be as simple as a word or as complex and as powerful as a form letter. You can even share your Textexpander codes with your co-workers, resulting in documents that have a consistent style across the company regardless of the author. Textexpander is available for individual, team, or enterprise use.

WEBSITE: https://textexpander.com/
FEATURES: https://textexpander.com/features/

Textexpander

COST

Free Trial Offer:	Yes
Subscription:	Yes
Price:	\$3.33 per month individual use \$7.96 per user per month for teams

AVAILABLE ON

Platform:	Windows
	iOS

SECURITY

2 Factor Authentication:	Yes
Data Security:	Encryption at storage and in transmission
Data Center:	

Other Features

Integration:	
Training:	Yes

About the Author

Andrew Zaso

Andrew Zaso has watched the growth of computer technologies evolve in business over the past 30 years. He began his career in the '90s running a mainframe system in the US Senate and was one of the first senate offices to deploy a local area network. His career has included work at the US Secret Service, Department of Homeland Security, US Food and Drug Administration, and the US Courts. He has worked in information technologies running application development shops, integrated financial systems, and managed computer data centers. His last position in the Federal Government was running the case management system for the US Courts as a Senior Executive. These systems included the case management system used by Bankruptcy, District, and Appellate Courts and the Federal Probation and Federal Defender system.

Andrew has a Bachelor of Science degree in Engineering from Boston University, an MBA from George Washington University, and a Master of Information Systems from Syracuse University. He also holds several IT certifications, including Project Management Professional (PMP), Cyber Security Certification: CISSP, CCSP. In addition to his professional certifications, Andrew has certifications from AWS and AZURE. Currently, Andrew currently works in the cybersecurity industry, developing systems that protect government agencies from cyber attacks.

CloudRDY LLC

This book is brought to you by CloudRDY, LLC, which offers a wide range of consulting services, combined with industry experience, to help grow your business. We partner with our clients from start to finish, focusing on their needs while producing new ideas, developing effective strategies, and designing high quality and scalable solutions.

Contact us to learn more. www.cloudrdy.com

20210402

www.ingramcontent.com/pod-product-compliance
Lightning Source LLC
LaVergne TN
LVHW041204050326
832903LV00020B/453
* 9 7 9 8 5 9 9 3 8 9 6 0 6 *